If I'm not willing ...
same amount
in getting
as I did when I was getting
high and trying to get high,
I will never recover!

SOME SAT IN
DARKNESS

SOME SAT IN DARKNESS

Spiritual Recovery from
Addiction and Codependency

❖

MIKE LEATHERWOOD
BRENDA LEATHERWOOD
DECLAN JOYCE
JOANNE RANDALL

DPI
DISCIPLESHIP
PUBLICATIONS
INTERNATIONAL

2 Sterling Road
Billerica, Mass. 01862
1-888-DPI-BOOK
Fax (978) 670-8485
www.dpibooks.org

Some Sat in Darkness

Printed in the United States of America

Cover design: Chris Costello
Interior design: Laura Root & Chris Costello

ISBN:1-57782-024-X

Brenda and I would like to dedicate this book to some very special people. First of all we would like to thank our parents, Eddie and Johnnie Leatherwood and Kelly and Dorothy Clemens, who taught us to have a heart for others. Next, we would like to thank Steve and Lisa Johnson, who helped us through the darkest period of our lives and without whose vision the chemical recovery (CR) ministry would not exist. Last, but not least, we would like to thank Don and Alice Peden, Sonny and Carolyn Sessions and the Louisville Church of Christ, who provided us with an opportunity to serve with them and learn how to help the suffering addict.

MIKE & BRENDA LEATHERWOOD

To Nancy, the love of my life.

DECLAN JOYCE

To Tom Randall: I have come to cherish everything about you deep within my heart. Thank you for encouraging me to share with others the hope we have found.

JOANNE RANDALL

Contents

Foreword 9

Introduction   Breaking the Chains:
               New York's Chemical Recovery Ministry 11

Chapter 1   Defining Chemical Dependency 15

Chapter 2   Converting the Addict 40

Chapter 3   Discipling the Addict 54

Chapter 4   Disciples and Alcohol
               To Drink or Not to Drink? 62

Chapter 5   No More Playing God
               The Serenity to Accept the Things
               I Cannot Change 75

Chapter 6   Intervention
               The Courage to Change the Things I Can 83

Chapter 7   Approaches to Treatment
               The Wisdom to Know the Difference 90

Chapter 8   Codependency Recovery
               The Resurrected Life—Part 1 105

Chapter 9   Codependency Recovery
               The Resurrected Life—Part 2 120

Chapter 10   My Husband Stopped Drinking
               So Why Am I So Unhappy? 145

Chapter 11   Starting a Chemical Recovery Group 157

Appendix 164

Notes 165

Bibliography 168

Some sat in darkness and the deepest gloom,
　　prisoners suffering in iron chains,
for they had rebelled against the words of God
　　and despised the counsel of the Most High.
So he subjected them to bitter labor;
　　they stumbled, and there was no one to help.
Then they cried to the LORD in their trouble,
　　and he saved them from their distress.
He brought them out of darkness and the deepest gloom
　　and broke away their chains.
Let them give thanks to the LORD for his unfailing love
　　and his wonderful deeds for men,
for he breaks down gates of bronze
　　and cuts through bars of iron.

Psalm 107:10-16

Foreword

It's not difficult for me to write a foreword to a book about the chemical recovery (CR) ministry. In fact, I've been waiting years for an opportunity to share what this remarkable group of people has achieved in the New York church.

Almost ten years ago, during a long airplane ride, I read an article in *Fortune* magazine that talked about the toll that drug abuse has taken on the business community in the U.S. The article estimated that a staggering forty percent of the employees in the top 500 companies in the country were, in one way or another, addicted. A little while after this, Mike Leatherwood, who at the time was leading the New Jersey sector of the New York church, came to Lisa and me and confessed the problems he had been having with alcoholism.

What these events, among others, helped Lisa and me to appreciate was that drug and alcohol addiction is not a problem that is limited to skid-row bums and strung-out, needle-park freaks, but reaches into every level of American society, and right into our own backyard. In fact, in the New York church at the time, it became apparent that substance abuse problems were the number one reason people were falling away from the church.

Just as we had done a little earlier with the inception of the daytime ministry to people in the arts and entertainment industry, Lisa and I began to try to figure out ways that we could help keep in the church a group of people who, left to their own devices, were going to have a hard time remaining faithful to the Lord. The result was what has become known as the CR ministry.

Contrary to some popular misconceptions that persist even to this day, the bottom line in CR is very intense discipling. I believe the CR ministry is the most outward-focused ministry in the church: Over three thousand people in New York have been baptized by people who have been helped by the CR ministry. Hundreds of families have been healed from the ravages of addiction. Many of our most prominent leaders in the NY church have become the type of leaders they have because of being part of the CR ministry. I believe that all over the world there are people who would be staying faithful if only we had ministries like this where they live.

The chemical recovery ministry is not a benevolent outreach program. It is not a social program. It is church. It is discipleship. With God, we have found the most effective way of dealing with drugs in the world. It is a unique ministry, and it hasn't just helped us in New York; it has saved thousands in other cities who I am confident would otherwise be lost. I believe the time is right for the CR ministry to become a presence all over the world. I believe this book will go a long way toward helping bring this about.

Steve Johnson
Lead Evangelist
New York City Church of Christ

Introduction

MIKE AND BRENDA LEATHERWOOD

Breaking the Chains

New York's Chemical Recovery Ministry

> I have become all things to all men, so that by all possible means I might save some.
>
> 1 Corinthians 9:22b

The New York City Church of Christ was planted with eighteen disciples in 1983. Within the first two years leaders Steve and Lisa Johnson realized that one of the major causes for disciples falling away from God was chemical dependency. Whether the substance was alcohol, cocaine, heroin, marijuana, nicotine or prescription drugs, people addicted to them were not remaining faithful. Something was missing in either converting or nurturing this group, and it had to be changed.

Anyone who knows Steve and Lisa knows that absolutely no time is wasted ruminating over problems. Their energy is spent finding an effective solution and implementing it as soon as possible. Hence the beginning of the chemical recovery (CR) ministry in New York. From its inception, the goal of the CR ministry has been to be an asset to church growth. First, the tide needed to be stemmed of those falling away, and then this enormous group with potential for much good needed to be channeled into useful service.

Historically, people have seen alcoholics and drug addicts as anything but an asset. Mention an alcoholic, and many think immediately of the stereotype of the skid-row bum. Talk about drug addicts, and many picture a heroin addict with a needle in his arm. At one point such stereotypes did hold some amount of truth. Before the drug revolution of the '60s the typical alcoholic was in his fifties to early sixties and pretty well burned out. But in the late '60s something significant happened. Mood-altering drugs, such as LSD and marijuana, were popularized. The widespread use of these and other drugs permanently changed the face of addiction. What we began to see in drug and alcohol treatment programs was a much younger population. The typical person in treatment today is in his late twenties to early thirties. Many have college degrees and have experienced a certain amount of success. They are, for the most part, gregarious and talented. The church in New York has not seen this population as high risk, but as an unredeemed resource. The typical drug addict today has great people skills and years of productive service ahead if he or she recovers. In fact, recovered addicts are some of the most grateful, most motivated and most effective disciples in the church.

God has always had a plan of recovery for chemical addiction as well as all the other messes we get ourselves into. This plan is seen clearly in the psalm from which we take the title of this book:

> Some sat in darkness and the deepest gloom,
>   prisoners suffering in iron chains,
> for they had rebelled against the words of God
>   and despised the counsel of the Most High.
> So he subjected them to bitter labor;
>   they stumbled and there was no one to help.
> Then they cried to the Lord in their trouble,

and he saved them from their distress.
He brought them out of darkness and the deepest
   gloom
and broke away their chains.
Let them give thanks to the Lord for his unfailing
   love
and his wonderful deeds for men,
for he breaks down gates of bronze
and cuts through bars of iron (Psalm 107:
   10-16).

The entire psalm describes the process of our turning away from God, the consequences of that decision, the coming to our senses and connecting of our pain with our actions, and finally the return to God and his deliverance. This is the plan presented in this book.

Over the past ten years, the New York City church has seen over 500 men and women graduate from the CR ministry and remain faithful to this day. These 500 disciples have been involved in Bible studies in which over 4,000 people have then been baptized into Christ. Such statistics dispel the myth that forming a CR ministry creates an inward focus. Currently, thirty-eight percent of these graduates serve in various leadership roles, including serving as evangelists and women's ministry leaders, regional and sector leaders, teen and children's ministry leaders, Bible Talk leaders and song leaders.

One of the biggest challenges facing the chemical recovery ministry is that we lose our best CR group leaders to the full-time ministry. This is a nice problem to have and is a true reflection of the power of God's Spirit, his plan to redeem us from an empty way of life, and his desire to give us a life filled with hope and purpose.

We believe the implications for your ministry are obvious. Many of you are in countries where drug addiction and alcoholism are a national stigma. Others of you are in small towns or rural areas. Wherever you are, drugs are a problem. When Brenda and I operated a halfway house in Kentucky, most of our clients were from Harlan County, a secluded rural area in the mountains of eastern Kentucky. Since approximately one out of every eight people we study the Bible with in the U.S. will be addicted to alcohol, there are really no churches that would not benefit from a chemical recovery ministry.

Just as the church has developed and matured in converting and discipling college students, teens, marrieds and young professionals, so our increased knowledge and maturity concerning chemical addiction will serve to advance the kingdom even further.

1

DECLAN JOYCE

Defining Chemical Dependency

The primary reason for having a CR ministry in New York has always been to help the church grow dynamically. Many people come into the kingdom with a background of drug and alcohol addiction. Once they have quit drugs and alcohol and become disciples, many try, after a period of sobriety, to drink normally again. Many end up getting drunk and then falling away. Many more get drunk but hang in there and eventually get sober and stay sober. But for years they are spiritually crippled and more of a liability to the kingdom than an asset. The purpose of the CR ministry is to break that destructive pattern and help young disciples get strong in the early months of their discipleship and live effective lives for God. CR was never intended to be a long-term pity party where weak disciples sit around sympathizing with one another about the hard lives they have led. Nothing could be further from the truth.

The extent of the drug problem in the US alone is immense:

> Since one out of four Americans lives with or is intimately connected to an alcoholic son, daughter, brother, sister, spouse or friend, it is safe to assume that you know one. Somewhere between five and ten percent of all adult Americans are alcoholics...

Whether the number of alcoholics is as low as five
million or as high as thirty-six million, or even higher,
every one of them affects an average of six other
people. In other words, well over one half of all
Americans are troubled somehow by this abuse.[1]

If the kingdom lacks the ability to effectively work with
this population, their chances for recovery are not good:
Typically ninety-six percent will die in their addiction, three
percent will recover, and one percent will be permanently
institutionalized (in psychiatric hospitals, prisons etc.).[2] This
is all the wisdom the world has to offer. However, because
of God's word and his Spirit, the kingdom can have a record
that completely contrasts that. In New York City, there are
approximately 5,000 disciples in the church. Of that number there are approximately 600 people in recovery from
drugs and alcohol who have either graduated from CR or
are currently in the program. Of those who have graduated,
ninety-six percent have remained sober. Only God could
produce statistics like this.

Most addicts that we study the Bible with approach the
church doubtful that they have a problem with drugs and
alcohol. If they do have a problem, however, and it is not
addressed early on, their chances of remaining faithful to
God are much reduced. Your first and most obvious task,
therefore, is to find out if the person you're studying with is
an addict. This is not as straightforward as it may sound:
Less than five percent of drug addicts conform to the skid-
row or needle-park stereotype. The other ninety-five percent are outwardly leading normal lives with spouses, families, jobs, and so on. Very few will admit they have a drug
problem, or even recognize the fact. Remember, it is in the
nature of addiction to hide itself not only from others, but
from the addict himself, through a process called denial. It's
possible to talk with an aged, institutionalized alcoholic or

drug addict who has lost everything as a result of his or her addiction, and be told with a straight face and the utmost sincerity: "I'm not an addict. I've never had any problem with alcohol or drugs."

So, simply asking someone whether or not they are an addict is not going to get you very far. Your job is to figure out specifically what involvement he has had with drugs and alcohol. In short, *how* did he use? How much? How often? How long? Which drugs? Did he continue to use in spite of the consequences? If you are dealing with a member of the church, did he continue to use after he became a disciple? Ask specific questions, not in a belligerent way, but in a direct way, out of concern. Be willing to push past any of his reluctance to answer. A tendency to waffle or be vague on his part is a fairly reliable bellwether of a drug problem.

Defining Chemical Dependency

As recently as ten years ago, bookstores stocked little or nothing in the way of books on addiction and recovery. Today, the average bookstore boasts a bewildering profusion of titles devoted to recovery and self-help, everything from *Getting in Touch with Your Inner Child* to *Practical Daily Meditations for Compulsive Shoppers*. The net result, apart from making a lot of people rich, has been a growing confusion as to what addiction and recovery really are. Is addiction a disease? Is it a neurological disorder? Is it a chemical imbalance? Am I even responsible for being an addict?

As with everything else, God wrote the book on addiction and recovery, and while breaking a drug habit is never easy, the actual business of defining addiction is very straightforward. In the middle of his letter to the Romans, the apostle Paul wrote a passage that will strike a strong and immediate chord with anyone who has ever struggled with addiction:

> We know that the law is spiritual; but I am unspiritual, sold as a slave to sin. I do not understand what I do. For what I want to do I do not do, but what I hate I do.... I know that nothing good lives in me, that is, in my sinful nature. For I have the desire to do what is good, but I cannot carry it out. For what I do is not the good I want to do; no, the evil I do not want to do—this I keep on doing....
>
> So I find this law at work: When I want to do good, evil is right there with me. For in my inner being I delight in God's law; but I see another law at work in the members of my body, waging war against the law of my mind and making me a prisoner of the law of sin at work within my members. What a wretched man I am! Who will rescue me from this body of death? Thanks be to God—through Jesus Christ our Lord! (Romans 7:14-25).

Why would someone, especially someone as spiritually mature and powerful as the apostle Paul, continue to struggle with something that, as is evident from this passage, he desperately wants to change? The answer: Enslavement. Powerlessness. Have you ever firmly decided to quit drugs or alcohol, yet continued to use? Have you ever decided to cut down on the number of beers you drank in an evening, but found yourself drinking as much as ever? An inability to follow through on decisions of this kind constitutes a loss of control, an enslavement. If you've ever made a decision to cut down or cut out your intake of drugs or alcohol, you made it for one reason only: They were beginning to cause you some problems, some pain or discomfort, and you decided that you needed to make some changes. A sound decision, and one that in most areas of life we are capable of following through on.

Normally, when something causes us pain, we stay away from it. About eight years ago, I ordered a bowl of chili in a New York restaurant. It gave me a fairly severe case of food poisoning, and for the next two days I never strayed more than ten feet from a bathroom. Since that day, I have never returned to that restaurant. Quite reasonably, I decided to stay as far away as possible from something that had caused me great pain. When it came to drugs, though, my power of reasoning seemed to desert me. When I used drugs, I would get ripped off, lose my money, feel physically sick and paranoid and be overcome with feelings of shame, remorse and self-hatred. In the last few months before I was finally willing to be open and honest, I had become isolated from my brothers and sisters and most importantly God—I had seriously jeopardized my relationship with my God. All of this together constitutes a really bad bowl of chili, and yet I kept on going back for more. Madness. Foolishness. Enslavement.

The reason many of us have difficulty defining addiction in these straightforward terms is that it runs directly counter to some very deeply held beliefs about drug addicts and alcoholics. For years, addiction was moralized by the religious and medical establishments: Addicts, according to conventional wisdom, just needed to desist from their wicked ways, clean up their acts and get a job like the rest of us. When treatment facilities of any kind began to appear, they tended to deal exclusively with people in the very last stages of addiction: the Bowery bum with his bottle of rotgut wine or the emaciated needle-park freak begging for spare change. Hence our popular notions of what constitutes an alcoholic or drug addict. While such people are indeed addicts, they are actually in the final stages of a cycle that may have begun ten, twenty or even thirty years earlier.[3]

Contrary to the beliefs of some, the Bible doesn't condemn the use of alcohol: Jesus turned water into wine at a wedding feast in Cana (John 2), Paul counseled Timothy to take a little wine for medicinal purposes, and the Old Testament has several positive references to the sensible enjoyment of wine. So using alcohol in moderation is not wrong. Drugs such as marijuana, cocaine, or heroin, however, are illegal, and we cannot use them in any amount and still please God.

Abuse of alcohol, more colloquially known as plain old drunkenness, is without question condemned by the Bible (Galatians 5:19; 1 Corinthians 6:12). The Bible is full of references to the evil effects of drunkenness, even strongly implicating it in the spiritual downfall of Israel.[4] It's true that some people can hold more alcohol than others, or metabolize alcohol at different rates depending on body weight. It's important, though, that we not use such reasoning to justify crossing the line from the use to the abuse of alcohol. Remember the apostle Paul's words: "the acts of the sinful nature are obvious" (Galatians 5:19). Each of us knows full well when we've crossed the line, however hard we may try to delude ourselves. Again, this is not to say that anyone who drinks has a problem with drunkenness. Many of us have come from religious backgrounds where *any* use of alcohol was severely frowned upon. Such unbiblical attitudes have been dispelled among most disciples today. But in matters of this kind, the danger always exists of the pendulum swinging too far in the other direction. We can easily foster attitudes that are far too liberal and cause others to stumble.

➤ Most people who continue to abuse drugs or alcohol will cross that line into addiction. There is no sudden drop off point, no blinding flash of light, no loud warning bells. Here is how it usually works: As a result of drug or alcohol abuse, we will have some bad experience, probably relatively minor, and will continue to use in spite of it. Drugs and alcohol have begun to mean more to us than avoiding pain. We have crossed the line. What can make this so deceptive and insidious is that we *seem* to have control because painful consequences don't happen every time. But the fact is that if we have lost the ability to predict with certainty the outcome of a particular episode of drinking, then we have lost control. Sometimes, especially in the early stages of addiction, we will use and relatively little will happen that's negative. Other times we will get drunk, embarrass ourselves, get a DWI (Driving While Intoxicated) citation, waste money, black out, lose a job, damage a relationship and so forth. As we continue to use, the consequences worsen as we sink deeper into the morass of addiction.

In order to justify behavior that causes us pain, we have to find something to blame the pain on, something that can take the rap for the unpleasant consequences we have received as a result of use. Then, as addiction progresses, our minds are occupied more and more with devising explanations for our irrational behavior.[5] Otherwise we would find ourselves constantly confronted with the need to quit. So we place the blame on our wives, our jobs, our socio-economic background, our families. Anything will do. This is why, when many of us have studied the Bible with people from a drug-addicted background, we have had tremendous difficulty motivating them to accept responsibility for their lives. Blame-shifting over the years has become their second nature.

In his book, *Understanding and Counseling the Alcoholic*, Dr. Howard Clinebell provides a list of questions used by the late psychiatrist, Robert Seliger, to assist a person in evaluating his alcohol use. Because addiction can be so deceptive, it may be helpful for you or someone you are working with to take this short quiz and do some self-assessment. A few yes answers could indicate a problem.

1. Do you lose time from work due to drinking?
2. Is drinking making your home life unhappy?
3. Do you drink because you are shy with other people?
4. Is drinking affecting your reputation?
5. Have you ever felt remorse after drinking?
6. Have you gotten into financial difficulties as a result of drinking?
7. Do you turn to lower companions and an inferior environment when drinking?
8. Does your drinking make you careless of your family's welfare?
9. Has your ambition decreased since drinking?
10. Do you crave a drink at a definite time daily?
11. Do you want a drink the next morning?
12. Does drinking cause you to have difficulty sleeping?
13. Has your efficiency decreased since drinking?
14. Is drinking jeopardizing your job or business?
15. Do you drink to escape from troubles or worries?
16. Do you drink alone?
17. Have you ever had a complete loss of memory as a result of drinking?
18. Has your physician ever treated you for drinking?
19. Do you drink to build up your self-confidence?
20. Have you ever been to a hospital or institution on account of drinking?[6]

Myths and Stereotypes

As mentioned above, there is a tremendous amount of confusion about drug addiction and treatment. In particular, there are a number of widely held myths and stereotypes that you should be aware of, both as a recovering addict or as one working with addicts.

Myth 1: "I Am Not Responsible" (or "The Devil Made Me Do It!")
The so-called "disease concept" of alcoholism, i.e. the notion that alcoholism is a disease, and hence, we are not responsible for it, gained popularity in the 1950s. At that time, the established church had failed the alcoholic, branding alcoholism as moral dissolution, denouncing it from the pulpit and generally offering no practical help. As a result, the moral component was gradually removed from the treatment of alcoholism, and it began to be seen more as a medical problem.

Especially influential in this respect was Dr. Elvin Morton Jellinek (we kid you not!), who, as a result of working with thousands of alcoholics, began to identify common symptoms and phases they went through as their addiction progressed. He graphed this process in a work known as the Jellinek Chart, which is still a useful tool for identifying addiction.[7] The Jellinek Chart is detailed at the end of this chapter. The deceptive thing about the "disease concept" is that it's half true: alcoholism, in some respects, resembles a disease in that it has, as Jellinek noted, specific symptoms and phases. It is not a disease in the normal sense, however, in that it is not something you catch and have no responsibility for. If we persist in abusing drugs and alcohol in spite of repeated warning signs, we will eventually reach a point where we are powerless. In most cases, though, it takes a lot of bad decisions to get there, and biblically we can get help and are even required to get help long before we cross the line into enslavement.

Myth 2: Willpower Works
All of us have the option to quit drugs or alcohol when we begin to see our sinful results. Once we have crossed the line into enslavement, however, we have lost that capacity, and it is only God who can help us. A slave has no control over his own destiny. The deceptive thing is that even the

most far-gone alcoholic or drug addict can stop *for a while*. The problem is they can never quit permanently. It brings to mind what Mark Twain said about quitting smoking: "It's easy; I've done it a hundred times." There is a world of difference between not using and actually recovering from addiction. Periods of abstinence only serve to strengthen the illusion that we are in control. True sobriety is being comfortable with not using.

Myth 3: "I'm Unique"

Addicts surround themselves with a system of defenses so sophisticated it can make Fort Knox seem like the Magic Kingdom.[8] One of the most common defenses is the insistence that the nature of their particular addiction is unlike any other. The purpose of this particular defense is, like all others, a desire to keep using. If the addict can convince himself (and others) that his drug problem is an extremely complex affair, rooted in childhood conflicts and ingrained in personality disorders, he has provided himself with a valid excuse to keep using. Furthermore, he can insist that no one else can help him, because they cannot relate to what he's been through. The Bible, however, teaches that "no temptation has seized you except what is common to man" (1 Corinthians 10:13). Every addict feels unique: None is. Accepting this truth is one of the most basic requirements for recovery. Many addicts will also insist that they can only be understood or helped by other addicts. Romans 7:14-21, however, teaches that we can all relate to addiction, because we have all understood what it means to be powerless over sin.

Myth 4: Every Addict Is on Skid Row

The hard facts tell us that only about five percent of all addicts conform to the skid-row typology: drinking rotgut wine, living in flophouses, sleeping in the street and so forth. The other ninety-five percent have steady jobs, families, and lives that are, from the outside at least, "normal." The basis of this particular myth, as mentioned earlier, is the treatment facilities of the 1950s, when virtually no one got into treatment until his addiction reached a chronic stage. Today, however, the typical person in recovery is much younger, better educated and has great people skills. He will also have a lot of years ahead of him if he can recover and build a great life as a disciple. Buying into the lie of the skid-row mind-set will keep us convinced that any ministry that includes large numbers of recovering addicts will be a weak one. It will also keep us from asking the right questions with "sharp" people, because we're assuming we know what an alcoholic or drug addict looks like. As a case in point, there are almost a dozen people on the full-time staff of the New York Church of Christ that are graduates of our CR ministry, including several who are leading sectors and regions.

Myth 5: Time Heals

This is one of the most subtle traps a recovering addict must avoid. After a period of abstinence, the mind begins to suggest that since sobriety has been attained and addiction seems to have become a thing of the past, a little controlled drinking might not be amiss. Indeed, it is often possible to "get away with" some limited drinking for several weeks, even months. Yet even a temporarily "successful" attempt by an addict to drink moderately will immediately plunge him into discontent and frustration because he will inevitably want more. Then because he has given himself a message that he can now drink normally, his pride will eventually trip him up and return him to a pattern of drinking that, if anything, is more severe than before. The Bible is clear that we should completely leave behind anything that has caused us to sin. For an addict to try a little controlled use of something that has led him into sin in the past is as absurd as someone who has had his life destroyed by sexual sin buying a copy of *Playboy* in order to just read the articles.

Myth 6: "I'm An Alcoholic, Not a Drug Addict"

In this book, we use the terms "drug" and "alcohol" more or less interchangeably. This is because there is no difference: The drug known as ethyl alcohol is one of the most destructive of all and should not be considered as belonging to a less serious category.[9] Withdrawal from chronic alcohol addiction is still a life-threatening situation during detoxification.

From the point of view of someone still actively using drugs, however, there is a difference. The mind is endlessly inventive in coming up with ways to bargain with addiction, and switching the drug of choice is one of the most common: "Okay, I accept that I have a problem with cocaine," the reasoning goes, "but I believe I can still use alcohol normally." When someone tries to use one drug as an acceptable substitute for another, one of two things invariably happens: (1) They end up becoming addicted to the substitute, or (2) the substitute sets them up to relapse into using their original drug of choice. In order to recover, the addict must accept that they are powerless over any and all drugs. Abstinence is the key.

Myth 7: "Why I Used Is Important"

Drug addicts are usually self-obsessed, self-absorbed people, more than happy to acquaint you with the exact series of circumstances, mishaps and bad breaks that were responsible for their drug problem.[10] But all of us who are addicts became so for one reason: We willingly and knowingly made a long series of bad decisions that ultimately led us to a point where we became powerless. No one forced us into it. We enjoyed drugs, we abused them, and eventually they enslaved us. Trying to offer any other reason for abuse is not only a justification, but it also will keep us from the frank admission of our own fault and blame that is a prerequisite for recovery. It's also dangerous in another respect: If an addict identifies a bad marriage as the reason for his drinking, for example, and after several months in the kingdom his marriage begins to improve, he will often conclude that he is now able to drink normally. In short, *why* the addict uses is not the issue; *how* the addict uses is what counts.

Myth 8: Fear Works

Sometimes an addict will temporarily stop using because of some particularly bad drug-related experience. However, fear never keeps anyone sober for long. I worked with a man in recovery who once woke up in an intensive care unit with wires taped all over his body. For the first few hours he was terrified. Before long, however, he tore the wires off his body, got off the bed, walked out of the hospital and went to get high. Pain works, fear doesn't.

Myth 9: Nicotine Is Not Serious

Nicotine is among the most dangerous of drugs and among the most addictive. From a spiritual standpoint, more people fall away from God as a result of nicotine addiction than any other addiction. In New York we've known plenty of heroin addicts who have been able to quit heroin but have been unable to stop smoking. Part of this can be explained by the fact that a smoker goes into withdrawal from nicotine after only twenty minutes. A single shot of heroin can last an addict a whole day, but a smoker begins to feel discomfort and the need to medicate after only twenty minutes. The facts speak most profoundly of all: In 1995, a total of just over 10,000 people died in the U.S. as a direct result of all illicit drug use. During the same period, over 400,000 people died as a result of nicotine-related illnesses.[11] People addicted to nicotine need help recovering just as much as any other group and should be referred to CR before they are baptized.

Reasons for Special Attention

Relapse

There are many reasons for devoting special attention to the needs of young disciples who have just emerged from years of drug and alcohol abuse. The first is the nature of relapse. If someone has a serious problem with lying, for example, and upon becoming a disciple they resolve to change but subsequently lie again, they simply need to resolve to try harder. If someone is a drug addict, however, a single recurrence of the sin can be devastating: They may never make it back. Time and again in New York we have seen this to be true. In fact, the principal reason for starting a CR ministry in the Big Apple was that substance abuse was the biggest single reason for people falling away from God.

Many Effects

Another reason for having a CR ministry is that addiction is such a devastating sin. It is what is known in medical circles as a primary problem, that is, a problem that must be dealt with first before any other area of life can improve. Addicts will typically seek help for their marriages, finances, etc., but nothing will change because the real root of the problem is not being addressed. No other sin has such destructive effects on so many areas of life: physical, mental, emotional, psychological, social, financial and spiritual. Therefore, addicts need specific help to stay sober in the early months of discipleship to stand a fighting chance of making it in the long term.

Detox Unit

Initial recovery often involves a stay in a detox unit, which focuses on the physical aspects of recovery. Great pains

are taken to protect a person during withdrawal. Most facilities provide medical supervision, plenty of rest in a clean,
safe environment and a balanced diet. Within three to
twenty-one days most people are over the physical effects
of withdrawal, although healing of the damage done to the
central nervous system may take several months.

Mental Recovery ☞

While much is made of the physical withdrawal from
drugs, in actuality recovering physically comes fairly quickly
for most people. Much more arduous is the process of recovering emotionally, mentally and spiritually. For several
years I conducted an informal study at the treatment center
I worked at in Louisville, Kentucky. Each week, I would ask
successive groups of approximately eighty men and women
how many of them ever thought they were crazy. Typically,
about ninety-eight percent of the hands would go up. Approximately sixty-five percent had been seen by a psychiatrist and had been given a psychiatric diagnosis. (This, of
course, is fine with the addict because, from his perspective, it provides confirmation that he is not an addict. He
now has professional assurance that the problem is a mental one, so he can continue to use drugs. This tends to be
more palatable to his family also, because there is much less
stigma attached to being mentally ill than to being a drunk
or a drug addict. Noteworthy is the fact that it can take as
long as six months of continuous sobriety in some cases
before an accurate psychological evaluation can be done.)
It is not surprising that many addicts eventually begin to
doubt their sanity: Imagine your very best thinking con-
tinually resulting in the same wretched failure and misery.

In the Parable of the Prodigal Son in Luke 15, the Bible
states: "When he came to his senses" he returned home (v.
17). Slavery to sin results in temporary "insanity." As

addiction progresses, the addict's mind becomes locked in an increasingly fierce battle with itself: the forces of reason and conscience battling it out with the forces of denial and rationalization. The mind is literally splitting in half, and eventually the strain begins to show.

Mental recovery, therefore, is a process which often takes many months. We have to learn how to think soberly. I have heard people at Alcoholics Anonymous (AA) meetings say, "When I first got sober, everything I thought was right was wrong." We must remember that the Bible is God's guide for recovering mentally from sin and its consequences. As we study the Bible and obey it, our thinking begins to clear up.[12] We begin to have our distorted thinking replaced with the truth about God, ourselves and others (Romans 12:1-2; Colossians 3:2; Ephesians 4:17-19, 22-23).

Emotional Recovery

Recovery also means recovering emotionally. Many people began to drink or use other drugs at age twelve or even earlier. As a result, instead of learning to deal with their emotions (i.e. resolving conflict, dealing with fear, anger, resentment or embarrassment), they simply medicated them, and as a result, never grew up emotionally. Now, equipped with the addict's genius for dissimulation, they appear to be fairly mature, well-adjusted twenty- or thirty-year-olds. But below the surface is an iceberg that can shipwreck their faith: emotional immaturity.

Obviously, we would study the Bible slowly with someone who is twelve years old because we realize that while they might understand the material intellectually, they need time to assimilate it emotionally. The same is true of those who began using drugs at an early age. For the most part these young disciples are emotionally twelve. They need time to learn how they feel, to look at the Scriptures and to talk to mature disciples who can help them develop appropriate emotional responses based on God's word. We can unknowingly frustrate young Christians by expecting more than they are capable of handling emotionally. It's important to be patient and anticipate such problems, like resolving conflict with other disciples. If we do not disciple young Christians considerately, we will set them up to relapse.

Recovering emotionally is a process that takes months or even years. However, because recovering people are typically grateful, eager and gregarious, they are sometimes moved too quickly into leadership. I have seen several very promising young Christians unable to emotionally handle the weight of leadership. Remember, if you give them time to grow up emotionally, they will be incredible leaders. If you do not, you might lose them entirely.

One good illustration of this principle can be seen in the requirements for certification as a chemical recovery counselor in the state of New York. You must have at least three years of continued sobriety before you can even take the exam. It is my opinion that the church would be better off giving recovering addicts at least a year to grow emotionally before assigning them to lead a Bible discussion group. Emotional recovery takes time, but it will happen if we are understanding, persistent and patient in our discipling of recovering addicts.

Spiritual Recovery

The spiritual aspect of recovery can often be the most elusive. Some people in recovery have a hard time with God because they define spirituality in strictly traditional religious terms and cannot imagine how "lighting candles and counting beads" could possibly have anything to do with recovery. Some doubt God's power to help due to their desperate appeals during periods of drunkenness and

God's apparent inability or unwillingness to respond. These addicts' enslavement to drugs have plunged them into a world filled with guilt, shame and remorse. They have not only violated their consciences, but in many cases have become so estranged from and bitter toward God that they cannot imagine God wanting anything to do with them.

Nonetheless, there is inherent in man a spiritual component, however hard he may try to escape it. Our conscience, that part of us that says "choose what is right," has been unable to function properly due to addiction. Our good intentions to pay bills, be on time for appointments and meet the needs of our families are never followed through on, and the result is increased shame and remorse. These feelings are amplified by the fact that at times the addict wants to quit, intends to quit, has quit dozens, hundreds of times, only to experience the insanity and intense wretchedness of his own powerlessness over and over again (Romans 7:14-21).

Other Problems

Addiction also devastates the addict financially, causing them to ruin their credit, pile up debts, ruin their career, etc. It can take years to get financially back on track. Likewise, relationships with friends, spouses and family also suffer. Some relationships are damaged so badly that trust must be painstakingly rebuilt over a period of years.

The Jellinek Chart

The Jellinek Chart, as mentioned previously, is a useful tool for helping people identify what stage of addiction they have reached. (See figure 1.[13]) Bear in mind, however, that not every alcoholic is going to go through all of these stages in this exact order. Also, although the chart was developed while working more or less exclusively with alcoholics, the dynamics for abuse of other drugs are practically identical. The following pages present an explanation of the symptoms and phases listed on the Jellineck Chart.

Prodromal (Early Warning) Stage

1. *First Blackout*—Blackouts are often confused with "passing out," i.e. a drug-induced state of unconsciousness. A blackout, however, is "alcoholic amnesia," a period of time

Jellinek Chart (Modified)
The Symptoms and Phases of Alcoholism

Prodromal Phase (Early Warning)	Acute Phase (Middle)	Chronic Phase (Late)
• First Blackout • Sneak Drinks • Preoccupied with Drinking • Gulp Drinks • Avoids Reference • Frequent Blackouts • Loss of Control (Which leads to the Acute Phase of Alcoholism)	• Alibis • Reproof • Extravagance • Aggression • Remorse • Water Wagon • Changes Pattern • Social Decay • Problems on the Job • Family Changes • Seeks Help	• Ethical Deterioration • Paralogical Thinking • Alcoholic Jealousies • Indefinable Fears • Tremors and Shakes • Psycho-Motor Inhibitions • Religious Need
Approximately 1 of 8 drinkers will become an alcoholic	• Resentments • Attempts Escape • Maintains Supply • Chain Drinking • Gross Physical And Psychological Changes • Prolonged Benders (Which leads to the Chronic Phase of Alcoholism)	Chronic Alcohol Addict
		Decreased Tolerance
Increased Tolerance		Vicious Cycle
Contact Phase		**Possible Outcomes** ▼ **Recovery** Insanity **Death**

Figure 1. The Jellinek Chart (Modified)

during an episode of drinking that you have no recollection of and cannot account for. An example would be having to be told the next day what happened at a party the night before, or coming to and not knowing where you left your car.

2. *Sneak Drinks*—The object of drinking is no longer social: The purpose is to get drunk, and the addict begins to develop a fear of sobriety. To this end, he will often arrive early for a drinking engagement to get in a couple of drinks before anyone else arrives or have a few drinks before leaving home. He might even offer to fix everyone else's drinks, so he can sneak a couple of extras while fixing theirs.

3. *Preoccupied with Drinking*—Drinking and getting drunk begin to occupy more and more of the addict's mind. Even when he is not actively using, he spends a lot of time thinking about it. It's increasingly becoming the center of his life.

4. *Gulp Drinks*—Another way to ensure quick intoxication is to ingest a lot of alcohol fast. Again, drinking is now solely about getting drunk.

5. *Avoids Reference*—At some level, the alcoholic recognizes that his drinking has become a problem. He therefore scrupulously avoids talking about what has become an uncomfortable topic and will quickly change the subject should anyone else bring it up or express concern.

6. *Frequent Blackouts*—Another warning sign that the alcoholic's drinking is getting out of control is when his blackouts become more frequent.

7. *Loss of Control*—This is an especially crucial stage, because it marks the dividing line between abuse and addiction. Previously, the addict has had the option of simply deciding to quit. At this stage, however, he will cross the

line into enslavement. This does not mean that he will lose control every time he drinks, but that he can no longer predict with certainty the outcome of any particular episode of drinking. Biblically, he is enslaved, and can no longer recover without the help of God and others.

8. *Increased Tolerance*—The body's tolerance for alcohol begins to increase: it takes more and more of the drug to get the alcoholic to the same high. Eventually, it takes huge amounts for him to simply feel normal.

Acute (Middle) Phase

1. *Alibis*—The need for the alcoholic to conceal his drinking now becomes more pressing, and he will enlist the help of drinking buddies, coworkers, etc. to conceal the extent of his drinking from those who are concerned. The classic image of this is the drunk in the bar asking the bartender to tell his wife on the phone that he left for home ten minutes ago. Alibis can also be lies the alcoholic tells himself, excuses he is making in order to avoid the truth.

2. *Reproof*—Despite such alibis and ploys, however, the addict begins to draw the anger of those around him who are being adversely affected by his drinking.

3. *Extravagance*—As a response to that anger, the addict will often respond with extravagant gestures, such as buying a new dress for his wife and new bikes for all the kids. This, of course, is not indicative of any real desire to change: It is simply a way of seeking to deflect criticism so he can get on with drinking undisturbed. A spouse's response, after several episodes of extravagance, might sound as follows: "How are we going to pay for all this stuff? I'd be happy if you just paid the light bill!"

4. *Aggression*—When extravagance inevitably fails, the next

stage is when the alcoholic gets angry every time the subject is brought up. Again, the purpose is to discourage any reference to the subject of drinking.

5. *Remorse*—The alcoholic at this point is beginning to experience some serious negative consequences and on some level recognizes this to be a result of his drinking. He may be overcome by feelings of remorse, shame and self-hatred, which he seeks to allay not by seeking help but by making some changes *on his own terms*.

6. *Water Wagon*—The first of these changes is to simply make a decision to quit, to "get on the wagon." This may be "successful" for a period of time, but because it is based on self-will rather than surrender, it ultimately fails.

7. *Changes Pattern*—The next option is to try to change the way he drinks. An alcoholic, for example, may resolve to swear off hard liquor and drink only beer, or to drink only at night, or only on the weekends. But because he is powerless over the substance at this point, any attempt to control drinking is fruitless, and the former patterns quickly resume.

8. *Social Decay*—The addict's social environment tends to be increasingly determined by his drinking. He becomes more withdrawn from "normal" society and either spends much of his time alone or in the company of others who drink the way he does.

9. *Problems on the Job*—Inevitably, job performance is adversely affected by his drinking. Typically, an addict will either move from job to job or, if he is good at concealing his drinking, be stalled in his career.

10. *Family Changes*—Family life cannot remain normal for the alcoholic. Either his family will begin to maladjust to

his drinking and become increasingly dysfunctional, or they will leave him altogether.

11. *Seeks Help*—The prospect of losing his wife and children is often enough for the alcoholic to begin to seek help, but for the wrong reasons. He may, for instance, seek marriage or financial counseling. Because his drinking is the true source of all his other problems, however, such counseling is inevitably doomed to failure.

12. *Resentments*—When all of his attempts at "seeking help" fail, the addict develops resentments against all those around him: "I've been trying to get help," his reasoning goes, "and nothing is changing. I've done all I can. The problem is my wife/boss/coworkers/friends."

13. *Attempts Escape*—The problems continue to mount. The addict may seek what is known as a "geographical cure," i.e. moving to another city, state or country in the mistaken belief that the root of his problems are other people, places and things. But because the source of all problems is the addict himself, this "geographical cure" is unsuccessful.

14. *Maintains Supply*—At this point, when all solutions appear to have failed, the addict begins to surrender to the addiction, giving up all attempts at change. He develops a morbid terror of being without his drug of choice and makes sure he always has an adequate supply.

15. *Chain Drinking*—Now the alcoholic progresses to the point of maintaining a constant supply of alcohol in his bloodstream. Hangovers become a thing of the past. The alcoholic is drinking to maintain some degree of normalcy.

16. *Gross Physical and Psychological Changes*—At this stage, overall health of the mind and body are seriously affected. The body is crumbling under the sustained assault of drugs

and alcohol, and the mind begins to split apart as the forces of reason and conscience are forced into submission by rationalization and denial.

17. Prolonged Benders—Life is now almost entirely given over to the drug. Sometimes whole days or even weeks are spent only drinking.

Chronic (Late) Phase

1. Ethical Deterioration—The addict's ability to reason has been so eroded at this point that he begins to lose his grip on right and wrong. He finds himself lying and stealing as a matter of course.

2. Paralogic Thinking—His thinking is no longer logical. "The problem is radio waves in my head," he may think. "If I can just hide from the radio waves, I'll get better."

3. Alcoholic Jealousies—The alcoholic is haunted by irrational jealousies. He accuses his wife of affairs, for instance, when there are absolutely no grounds for doing so.

4. Indefinable Fears—He becomes possessed by a pervading sense of dread, fearful at every moment that something awful is about to happen. He hides in his room, peeking out of the windows, plagued by paranoia.

5. Tremors and Shakes—Alcohol is beginning to render the body toxic. Tremors and shakes are a result of alcohol poisoning.

6. Psycho-Motor Inhibitions—Mind and body are no longer able to communicate. Simple moves such as stepping onto a curb may become difficult. The body is losing its ability to function normally.

7. Religious Need—The alcoholic typically gets involved in "revolving-door religion," going in and out of religious mission houses for a day or two at a time. Take a look at the "Bowery" section of your city, and you will probably find many mission houses side-by-side with flophouses and liquor stores. What is needed at this point, however, is a sustained physical, mental and spiritual recovery effort. The quick, mission religion is always ineffective.

At the end of this cycle the alcoholic's condition is chronic. His body begins to lose its ability to process alcohol, as liver damage becomes near-fatal (Decreased Tolerance). The only possible outcomes at this point are recovery, insanity or death.

2

DECLAN JOYCE

Converting the Addict

One day during the freezing winter of 1985, Terry P. sold his shoes for a single hit of crack. Miles from home, he had to take the subway back barefoot, drawing amused looks from his fellow subway riders. For Terry, the shame and remorse he felt that day was enough to finally make him surrender. Today, he has a beautiful wife and son, is a Bible discussion group leader, a mainstay of the New York church's CR ministry and is in his last semester of college.

John H. spent the better part of two decades as a heroin addict, making a living by stealing car parts and selling them back to crooked car dealerships. One night, on New York's Lower East Side, he jumped out of a second-story window in the dark to avoid arrest. Today, he is a Bible discussion group leader and a mainstay of the CR ministry.

The stories above are just two of literally hundreds of tales from our brothers and sisters in New York's CR ministry. Hundreds of people who have been freed from a paralyzing enslavement to drugs and alcohol have gone on to become leaders at various levels in the church's ministry and are an invaluable resource in helping the church grow.

The key to this type of success is knowing how to work effectively with people from this background. Helping addicts is fairly straightforward, but doing it wrong is even easier. Truly nothing is more frustrating and fruitless than trying to help an addict in the wrong way. In this chapter we will outline some basic guidelines in working with addicts. If you learn to work with addicts smartly, they will become a major asset to your church, not a hindrance.

Building Relationships

As with anyone you study the Bible with, a deep personal relationship is crucial. This is especially true with addicts, who are typically very secretive about themselves and live very isolated lives. Trying to rush someone through the necessary Bible studies that lead to conversion will inevitably result in your missing things that will help you identify if they need spiritual help in the area of drug abuse. It is wise to take the time to adequately assess whether they exhibit any of the warning signs listed below.

Don't Be Naive! Even disciples with extensive histories of drug abuse sometimes forget just how pervasive addiction is. Remember, almost everybody uses drugs to some extent, and as many as one in seven are addicted.

Evidence in the Home—Visit their homes. What kind of house does he keep? Don't be a super-sleuth, but be shrewd and be concerned. If someone has a living room full of lava lamps, an ashtray full of "roaches" (not the bugs, but the end of marijuana joints), a medicine cabinet full of prescription painkillers and a bookcase full of the works of J.R.R. Tolkien, you just might be on to something!

Habitually Late—Not everyone who shows up late for church or a Bible study is a drug addict (if they were, we would really be in trouble!), but if you *are* dealing with someone with a drug problem, you will not get far before you have a cancellation or more likely, a "no-show." I was late for most of my studies and did not show up for a few. The cause was invariably drug-related: either I was using drugs, or recuperating from using them.

Erratic Work Attendance—This is a common trait among addicts. Fridays they tend to leave early or not show at all because they began their weekend a day early. Mondays they won't show because they are still nursing hangovers or are sleep-deprived from staying up all weekend doing drugs.

Health/Legal/Marriage Problems—Addiction leads to problems in all these areas. He or she may be involved in marriage counseling, financial counseling, or a health regimen. Typically, an addict will seek help for all problems rather than the addiction itself. None of them are effective, of course, because the primary problem is still not addressed.

Financial Problems—Drug problems also devastate us financially, ruining our credit and causing us to run up huge bills. Eventually, all our money is going to drugs, and there is little left for anything else. If someone has a well-paying job but nonetheless seems to be always broke, chances are the reason is drug-related.

Nomad Living Pattern—At some point, almost every addict will seek what is known as a "geographical cure," i.e. moving to a different state, city or even country to try to escape drug problems. Some keep up this pattern for years, never staying in one place too long. Geographical cures are rooted in the mistaken belief that the cause of a drug problem is other people, other places and other things. Of course, the problem is always the addict himself, and after a brief period of relative calm, his problems always reappear.

Job Type—Certain jobs are favored by drug addicts, because they lend themselves to the addict life-style: a bartender, for instance, has easy access to alcohol. A pharmacist has easy access to painkillers. Working as a waiter/waitress is also popular because it provides money for drugs on a day-to-day basis in the form of tips. Self-employed jobs, such as house-painting, plumbing and landscaping, are popular because the schedule is flexible: You can use drugs whenever you want. Most favored of all is dealing drugs, although the dangers involved keep many from this option. Many addicts in nine-to-five jobs will routinely turn down promotions because they are able to do enough work in their present position to avoid being fired and still have plenty of time left over to drink on the job.

Never Finishing Things—As addiction progresses, more and more activities get relegated to the sidelines. Drug addicts, therefore, typically don't complete or sustain anything, be it college, work projects, personal projects or relationships.

High Frequency of Job Changes—Drug addiction makes it difficult to function well at work. As a result, the addict is either frequently fired, or frequently quits a job when either his work performance is challenged or when he sees a dismissal coming.

Physical Appearance—Physical signs are usually more obvious, but even these are missed: slurred speech, red eyes, smell of alcohol and so on.

Poor Comprehension—Years of consistent drug use take their toll on the brain and body. Poor mental comprehension and poor retention often result. An inability to retain or process information is also common. Our advice in this instance is: Give people time. Most people are not this far gone, but some do need a few months of sobriety before they can seriously comprehend what is involved in the life of a disciple. Some of the most difficult cases of poor comprehension are a result of solvent abuse, typically among young, white, blue-collar males. Solvent abuse (glue-sniffing, paint-huffing, etc.) results in an intense short-term high which quickly results in irreversible brain damage.[1] Typically, people from a background of serious solvent abuse are capable of doing exactly what you ask of them but are unable to reason. This has obvious effects on how quickly they can understand discipleship, let alone put it into practice.

Prescription Drugs—Not all addictive drugs are illegal: prescription drugs such as Percodan, codeine, etc., can be overprescribed by doctors and result in addiction. We need to be on the lookout for people that have access to almost unlimited supplies of prescription drugs, such as medical professionals and veterans. Prescription drug addiction often begins innocently as a result of seeking relief for severe back pain, stress or chronic illness. However, it is addiction nonetheless. Be on the lookout for people who have some of these conditions and are seeing several doctors.

Lying—Drinking and drugging makes you a grade-A pathological liar. You have to lie to maintain a steady supply of drugs. And the problem has gotten worse because the lies so often go unchallenged. You will help an addict out immeasurably if you refuse to accept lies. Ask specific questions; follow through on your hunches. If things don't add up, there is a reason. It may be drugs.

Constant Blame Shifting—As problems mount as a result of addiction, the addict feels an increasing need to find scapegoats for his behavior. Otherwise he is faced with increasingly compelling evidence of the need to quit. The result is a strong tendency to blame problems on spouses, bosses, or families and a reluctance to take responsibility for his actions.

Above all, pray! No matter how perceptive you are, you will miss some things if you rely on your own wisdom. Remember, being an addict means being deceitful. In many cases it has become second nature. Addicts are also some of the most winning, personable people you will ever meet (though this certainly does not apply to all of them!), because the addict life-style demands that they be able to talk their way out of trouble. Don't assume they are above pulling the wool over your eyes. Time and again when I have relied on my own wisdom in dealing with addicts, God has humbled me and reminded me of my need for him.

Who Can I Help?

When someone has received negative consequences as a result of using drugs and has nonetheless continued to use, they are powerless. There is no other explanation. We frequently illustrate this with what we jokingly refer to as "The Parable of the Broccoli." If, every time you ate broccoli, you got sick, blacked out, spent much more money than you intended to, got in trouble with the law and experienced adverse effects in your marriage, would you continue to eat it? Presumably not. Yet that was what we were willing to do when it came to drugs.

Once you have identified that someone has a drug problem, the second, and more important, question arises: Can you help him? In the movie *Rudy*, a kindly priest tells the eponymous hero that in all his years as a priest, he has learned two things: "There is a God, and I'm not him." There is a lot of wisdom in that statement. In almost ten years of working with drug addicts, I have experienced a considerable amount of frustration and in retrospect, I am convinced that almost all of it can be traced to the fact that I had not yet learned this lesson.

I am only effective in working with addicts when I realize that there are certain people I can help and certain people that I am completely *unable* to help. The most profound biblical illustration of this point is found in Luke 15:

Jesus continued: "There was a man who had two sons. The younger one said to his father, 'Father, give me my share of the estate.' So he divided his property between them.

"Not long after that, the younger son got together all he had, set off for a distant country and there squandered his wealth in wild living. After he had spent everything, there was a severe famine in that whole country, and he began to be in need. So he went and hired himself out to a citizen of that country, who sent him to his fields to feed pigs. He longed to fill his stomach with the pods that the pigs were eating, but no one gave him anything.

"When he came to his senses, he said, 'How many of my father's hired men have food to spare, and here I am starving to death! I will set out and go back to my father and say to him: Father, I have sinned against heaven and against you. I am no longer worthy to be called your son; make me like one of your hired men.' So he got up and went to his father" (Luke 15:11-20).

When I was finally ready to get sober, it was because the pain of using had become greater than the pain of not using. I did not wake up one morning, gaze at the glory of the rising sun and think, "You know, the world is just such a beautiful place, and here I am messing it all up with my nasty drug habit. Doggone it, it's time I got help." I would like to able to tell you that this was the case, but it was not. I got into recovery when the pain of the physical, emotional and spiritual consequences of my using became so intense that it ate through all my pride and I "came to my senses."

So it was with the lost or prodigal son in Luke 15. The indignity of longing to eat pig food (an abhorrent image to a Jewish audience), the physical pain of hunger, the emotional pain of remorse, finally brought him to a point where he was surrendered, where he was willing to be a "hired man." He was willing to get help, not on his terms, but on God's. Any attempt to intervene in this man's life before he came to his senses would have been not only fruitless, but intensely frustrating.

Even the secular world recognizes this. Consider this excerpt from Chapter 5 of *Alcoholics Anonymous*, the bible of AA:

> If you have decided you want what we have and are willing to go to any lengths to get it—then you are ready to take certain steps.
>
> At some of these we balked. We thought we could find an easier, softer way. But we could not. With all the earnestness at our command, we beg of you to be fearless and thorough from the very start. Some of us have tried to hold on to our old ideas and the result was nil until we let go absolutely.[2]

If you try to help an addict before he has reached the point of surrender, you will do him nothing but harm. In the Parable of the Lost Son, one of the keys to his surrender is found in verse 16: "but no one gave him anything." By having no one in his life who was willing to bail him out and rescue him from the consequences of his sin, the young man was able to "hit bottom." Had he had the intercession of a "kindly" friend at this point, he would never have made it back to his father.

Recognize and accept your limitations. Sometimes the most loving thing you can do is let go and let someone experience all the consequences that his willful, selfish way of life will inevitably bring him. Even God made no attempt to intervene in the young man's life. When he had come to his senses and surrendered, though, God was waiting with open arms. Likewise, you can only help people who have reached a point of surrender. Surrender is identified by a willingness to do anything "the master" requires, a willingness to be "a hired man." Try to help people before they have reached this point, and you will end up isolating them from the one thing that can bring them to a point of surrender.[3]

One of the most reliable ways to tell if someone is truly surrendered is whether he listens to advice from mature spiritual people, especially those who have years of sobriety under their belt, and follows that advice closely, not altering it into a more palatable form. Give an addict you are working with some specific, measurable things to do, and see if they follow direction accurately.

Recently, a brother in New York who had been very slow to respond to treatment and had repeatedly been late for CR groups was asked to do a 1,000-word essay on why being late for group would endanger his sobriety. At the next group he showed up with a 900-word essay. That might seem like a pretty good effort, but in reality, it was symptomatic of his problem: He took advice and altered it into something else—what he wanted to do. Remember, someone who has hit bottom will go to any lengths to change.

A further warning for all of us, and especially for the addict: There is a world of difference between saying we are going to do something and actually going ahead and doing it. Remember, deceit is part of the addict's life-style, so believe *what he does*, not what he says. Early in recovery, what an addict says has no value. This is not judgmental. It is a recognition of the fact that years of use has resulted in a pattern of deceit that can only be broken by a refusal to accept words as a substitute for actions.

Figure 2 illustrates very clearly what invariably happens when you try to help an addict who has not yet reached a point of surrender.

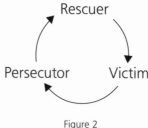

Figure 2

When you pour time and energy into someone who is not ready to change, you "rescue" or "enable,"[4] that is, you isolate him from the logical consequences of his drug use and thus rob him of the only thing, namely pain, that will help him come to his senses. When our rescuing is ineffective, we often simply try to help more, pay more of the addict's bills, field more phone calls, buy more groceries. As disciples, this is often done with good intentions, in the belief that it's what Jesus would do.

Eventually, as you continue to try harder and harder to change someone who, ironically, now has less and less motivation to change, you get angry. You begin to feel like a victim: "I've spent all this time and effort to help this guy, and he is just incredibly ungrateful." Rescuers become victims one-hundred percent of the time. Now you are angry, and you strike out at what you believe is the reason for your anger: the addict. You become a persecutor. Intolerant and less-than-loving attitudes take the place of your former misplaced concern. The addict is hurt, or at least acts hurt, wondering how someone who used to be so kind has suddenly become so cruel. He will often use this hurt as an excuse to use again. You in turn feel guilty, and resolve to try to be loving and kind again. The cycle is complete: You begin to rescue once more.

All of this is not to say, of course, that any addict should be treated with contempt or a lack of love simply because he has not yet hit bottom. Even if someone is not yet at a point where he is surrendered, I always affirm my concern for him and my willingness to help, but not on his terms. I have learned the hard way that I am unable to help an addict until he is willing to accept help on God's terms.

For example: If someone were to call me at 1:00 A.M. and tell me that he had gone to buy drugs, gotten arrested, hauled off to jail and now wanted me to come bail him out, I would say no. What I would do is offer to pray with him over the phone, bring his toothbrush and his Bible the next morning and so on. Going down and bailing him out would isolate him from the pain that will help him hit bottom. I would be acting as a worst enemy, not as a friend.

When Studying the Bible

When I started coming to church in the spring of 1986, my motivation was simple enough: I was miserable, and I wanted to not be miserable anymore. I had no notion of repentance, of change, or of personal responsibility. Most drug addicts will start attending church for similar reasons. They are not looking for a way to do God's will, but are looking for rest, for release. And God has indeed provided me with that in abundance, yet he did not do it in the way I had expected or wanted him to. I essentially wanted to sit back and watch God transform my life, to reap the benefits but take no active part in the process.

Drug addiction makes you self-obsessed, self-focused, deceitful, and a chronic blameshifter. Not exactly qualities that make for good discipleship! So when you sit down to study the Bible with people from drug-addicted back-grounds, these are the qualities you most likely have to help them overcome.

One point you will need to be especially careful about is repentance: Teach very clearly and specifically the differ-ence between worldly and godly sorrow.

> Godly sorrow brings repentance that leads to sal-vation and leaves no regret, but worldly sorrow brings death. See what this godly sorrow has pro-duced in you: what earnestness, what eagerness to clear yourselves, what indignation, what alarm, what longing, what concern, what readiness to see justice done. At every point you have proved your-selves to be innocent in this matter (2 Corinthians 7: 10-11).

Look for alarm, urgency, and a willingness to change (again based on actions, not words!). Don't agree to baptize people simply because they look like they are sorry. Addicts are usually filled with remorse, but remorse is not the same as repentance. Repentance is proven by deeds (Acts 26:20). If your church has a chemical recovery ministry, are they will-ing to be a part of it? Are they willing to write a thorough and honest journal?

For the uninitiated, the journal, which forms the back-bone of the recovery process in our CR groups, consists of the following three points: (1) what drugs they used, (2) what happened when they used them (i.e., the conse-quences), and (3) how they felt during and after the conse-quences. They should record every episode they can re-member, from the first time they used until the last time they used. They won't remember every instance, but they should not purposely leave out anything they do remem-ber. The goal of the journal is to help addicts connect pain with drug use. This will help them to hit bottom and ultimately to surrender to their powerlessness to alcohol and other drugs.

When someone reads his journal, everyone else in the CR group is expected to listen respectfully and intently. We are listening for surrender, that is, for a person to associate the pain in his life with using drugs and for a willingness to go to any lengths for God's help. We are listening to hear if he will glamorize, justify, rationalize or blameshift his drug use. We suggest that the journal be written as part of the sin and repentance study and be read in the CR group, if you have one. Otherwise, whoever he is studying the Bible with should go over it with him. If he is not willing to do these things, he is not yet surrendered, no matter now much he may protest to the contrary.

Deal with these issues before you baptize someone, not after. You are liable to meet resistance: When it was first suggested that I attend CR, I was terrified. Expect to be cajoled, bargained with, mollified and manipulated, but do not compromise. You and the addict will pay for it later if you gloss over his drug problem. You are up against the dread forces of denial, a defense mechanism designed to enable us to hold onto something that we deem necessary to our happiness or survival. Sometimes this is by conscious design, sometimes not. The person who is addicted to drugs and alcohol has already crossed the line from desire to need.[5] Remember, people who have a repentant spirit will go to any lengths to change. In New York, we have worked very hard to educate the full-time staff about CR, and they have always been incredibly supportive. Even so, occasionally someone manages to slip in under the radar and is baptized without the subject of CR coming up or being dealt with properly. The result is always bad and is sometimes disastrous.

Addicts are not in a special category. There are no "different rules" for them when it comes to basic biblical teaching about discipleship, repentance and commitment. However, just as with teens, campus students, the physically challenged and so on, we have come to recognize the need for specialized ministries. It is our firm conviction that meeting the specific needs of people from a background of drug and alcohol addiction will ensure that they become an asset to the ministry, not a burden, and more importantly, will ensure that they remain faithful till the end.

3

DECLAN JOYCE

Discipling the Addict

A strong relationship with God is essential to staying sober. For the addict, sobriety and remaining faithful are the same thing. The CR ministry in New York works hard at bringing home this point to disciples young in the faith and early in recovery. However, since a typical CR meeting takes place once a week and lasts an hour and a half, it is crucial that the young disciple is given the help he needs for the other 166 and a half hours of the week. This is primarily the responsibility of the discipling partner. Discipling the addict means putting together a spiritual aftercare program to help prevent relapse. Experience in the CR ministry tells us there are common guidelines that can help people early in recovery build a great relationship with God and ensure their continued sobriety:

Disciple through God's word—Help disciples early in their recovery understand that counseling from the world (AA and so on) is not what they need, but rather a growing knowledge of the Scriptures. Be confident that you, as a discipling partner, are "competent to instruct" because you are using God's word (Romans 15:14).

Expect emotional immaturity—Addiction stunts your ability to deal with emotional difficulties and problems. Because the life of a disciple demands emotional maturity, people are very susceptible to relapse in the early stages of recovery. It is almost a Catch-22 situation: Addiction robs you of the very qualities you need most to recover from it. Yet, there are two very effective ways to help people grow emotionally.

First, help them identify and deal with their emotions by writing down some basic feelings (i.e. mad, sad, glad, afraid, embarrassed), then looking up some scriptures on how to deal with those emotions. Suggest they memorize these passages or write them down on index cards for easy reference. Second, help them to use the Scriptures to train themselves to think and act in godly ways (1 Timothy 4:7). Help them to see that very often we have to think or act in a way other than how we may be feeling (Mark 14:32-41).

Ask questions—Another useful step in helping people identify what they are feeling is simply asking a lot of questions. Ask out of genuine concern, "Services went a little long today, how did you feel about that?" "Your friend was studying the Bible and decided he didn't want to be a disciple. Does that shake your faith?" "We talked at church tonight about a special missions contribution. Did you feel strange about that?" "I hear that sister that you liked doesn't feel the same way you do. Do you feel hurt?" Be sensitive to those times in a person's life when he is really susceptible to dealing with pain by using drugs or alcohol again. Be aware of Satan's schemes and ask questions. "Are you feeling sad?" "Are you feeling angry?" "What are you feeling?" You will probably be told, "I don't know." Emotional maturity cannot be aped; it must be learned the hard way. Help people understand that a lot of humility and willingness to learn is required if they are going to emotionally recover.

Encourage openness—Deceit is the first step toward relapse, and if the addict doesn't talk openly about what they

I need to talk about what I feel and all my crazy thoughts (no matter how illogical) so that I Do not become controlled by those feelings.

feel, that's deceitful. Al Baird wrote recently in an *LA Story* editorial that "Every disciple should have at least one relationship in the church that is so close that we can be totally real without fear of rejection."[1] Be that person for the addict. Remember, you're dealing with someone who has a lot of strange, unusual and uncertain feelings (or are convinced they do). Be sensitive. Rebuking someone early in recovery because his thinking is not correct will only exacerbate his feelings of isolation.

A couple of years ago in New York, a brother early in recovery was informed that there was an all-church meeting at Madison Square Garden the following week. He looked aghast, then quietly asked, "Is it about me?" He honestly thought the whole New York church was getting together to publicly renounce his sin. However off the mark his thinking may have been, it was real. Feelings are real, and talking about them needs to be encouraged. As we talk with the addict about his feelings, he will find it easier to not be controlled by them. On the other hand, the best way to be controlled by feelings is to not talk about them.

Encourage Humility—One key sign of relapse is prideful and argumentative behavior. When disciples early in recovery stop listening and taking advice, the alarm bells should start ringing. When pride goes up, sobriety invariably goes out the window.

Conflict Resolution—You will also need to teach people how to resolve conflict. Unresolved conflict is second only to pride as a major cause of disciples relapsing. Matthew 5:23-24 and Matthew 18:15-16 are therefore crucial for young disciples. *Alcoholics Anonymous*, the primary text of AA, says that the biggest single cause of relapse is resentment toward others. Help them learn to deal biblically with such resentments.

Expect Mental Dullness—If someone has smoked dope every day for ten years, they will experience mental sluggishness. Be patient: Some people just need time to come out of the fog.

Know Relapse Triggers—Alcoholics Anonymous uses the acronym H.A.L.T. to denote four conditions that can be triggers for relapse early in recovery: hungry, angry, lonely and tired. While there are times that disciples need to "push through" in spite of these things, we need to be cautious of pressuring people early in recovery.[2]

Adjust Their Focus Outward—Help people to be outward-focused. Using drugs has made them very inward and self-obsessed. When I had hurt someone through my using in the past, I was less worried about making amends than I was about the remorse and bad feelings that I was having as a result. Such experiences can easily hook young disciples back into using. Help get people out of that cycle of self-obsession by getting them into Bible studies, serving others and anything that will help them put the needs of others before themselves. Jesus said that he came to serve, and we have to help the recovering addict to be more like Jesus (Philippians 2:3-9; Mark 10:45).

Daily Fellowship—Help people early in recovery stay in touch with other disciples every day. Hebrews 3:13 is crucial for all new disciples, and especially those with a past of addiction. 1 Peter 5:8 teaches that Satan preys on the weak. Chemically dependent people usually do not know how to bond very well, so do not assume that they will make friends easily and not have to deal with feelings like awkwardness and isolation. Almost a year after I started coming to church, I was hanging out with some brothers and sisters after a Sunday church service. Suddenly, I began to be aware of feeling strange for some reason, and as I stood there in a group of people I gradually put it together: I was feeling at ease. It had taken almost a year for me to feel at home with people, and the feeling was so new to me that at first I didn't even recognize what it was.

Spiritual Household—Encourage people to be in a healthy spiritual environment, meaning stable households with Christian brothers or sisters. Otherwise they will continue to be at risk. Can you imagine trying to recover from open-heart surgery in the bathroom of a Greyhound bus station? Neither can people recover spiritually by going back to old friends, places and things. We must help set them up for success, not failure.

Never Assume—Do not assume anything. Do not assume that young Christians will not have an urge to use or won't get calls from old drug buddies. Do not assume that they won't have difficulty handling money or will find dating in the kingdom to be easy.

Time with God—Teach people the importance of a great relationship with God. They may know that they cannot use drugs anymore, but a lot of times they do not translate continuing sobriety into a great relationship with God. Teach the concept of repentance: not simply stopping the bad, but replacing it with the good. If they do not have a great time with God every day, sooner or later they're going to get weak and vulnerable.

"It's a CR thing; you wouldn't understand"—Do not fall for the line of reasoning that states you cannot relate to the addict unless you have had a drug or alcohol problem yourself. You may never have used drugs, but there is probably some sin that you tried unsuccessfully to change for years. Remember that the problems that the addict is dealing with are first and foremost spiritual. The Bible teaches that no temptation will seize us but what is "common to man" (1 Corinthians

— The Desire to get high or give in to impurity is *Just* a feeling. Take it to God in prayer !!

Discipling the Addict   59

10:13). We have all been enslaved to sin, so we can all relate to the feelings of enslavement and powerlessness that addicts deal with early in recovery (Romans 7:14-21).

Cockiness—Help people deal with overconfidence (1 Corinthians 10:13). Satan left Jesus for a time, but he came back (Luke 4:13). The same is true for recovering addicts. Help them avoid this trap. Just because they do not feel like using today doesn't mean they will not tomorrow. When people have been clean and sober for a while, there's a real tendency to become overconfident and to feel like they've put drugs or alcohol behind them forever. There are no short cuts to recovery, though. Reading their CR journal periodically is a useful way to help people stay in touch with who they are without God. Remember, the addict *will* have a desire to use again. Our responsibility is to teach them what to do when that happens. They need to take it to God. A desire to get high is a feeling, and if they pray long enough, the feeling will pass. Teach them to persist in prayer until they feel better and the desire leaves. As they pray, have them recite the scriptures they have memorized. The second thing to do is to call a mature brother or sister and work through the temptation. A smart idea is having easy access to both their daytime and evening phone numbers.

Fun—Teach them to have fun. Encourage them to live full and productive lives. Most healthy and enjoyable activities fall by the wayside when we are using, or are so adapted to our using that they are altered beyond recognition: We never really went fishing; we sat in a boat with a beer cooler. We never really played golf; we sat in a golf cart and drank. We didn't really go to rock concerts; we just used drugs to music. Learning to do these things sober is really like starting over again.

Frequent Accountability—Do not fill out a checklist, but ask them specific questions out of genuine concern. Ask people how they use money, how they spend time, etc. An unplanned Saturday night when the rest of the church is out on dates, for instance, is asking for relapse. Do not plan everything for them, but help them learn to think and plan for themselves in order to avoid falling prey to Satan's schemes.

Encourage—Be encouraging. Let people know that you believe in them. When I got sober, I had people in my life who believed in me, even though by most standards I was a fairly hopeless case. Do not hold back from telling the truth though; real disciples will always stay and work through whatever they need to.

Periods of Temptation—Be aware of critical periods when people are most susceptible to wanting to use: holidays, funerals, visits to the dentist (a "legitimate" excuse to use pain-killers!), illnesses, pay days, weekends. Also, for reasons we do not fully understand, three, six and eleven months after getting sober are typically times of great risk for relapse. Be especially vigilant during these times.[3]   *2.3 weeks*

Grieving—Help people through grief issues. When an addict becomes a disciple, they have to face a myriad of losses. For so long they have medicated the pain of funerals, lost friendships, bad decisions, wasted opportunities. Now they are faced with having to deal with all that pain at the same time, without medicating. Help them learn to deal with the grief by relying on God's word. Remember that grief is a process (denial, anger, bargaining, depression, acceptance) and takes time.[4]

Team Player—Teach people to work as a team. Addiction isolates us, so when we become disciples, we need help learning to work together. Encourage people to be involved

Ask people to Pray with me when I'm tempted to be impure.

[handwritten: Prioritize CR, Purity Group, and Quiet times! If I wont invest the Time and effort into being Sober then I'll never be Sober!]

in church-sponsored sporting events, double dating, being an active part of a Bible discussion group, and so forth.

Gratitude—Help people to stay grateful and thankful for small victories. For instance, in New York, getting a driver's license back has, in many cases, taken several years of concentrated effort: paying old parking tickets, taking subways, taking defensive driving courses, etc. God gives it all back to us, in his own time. Do not expect too much, too soon, without effort. Be grateful. *[handwritten: - Thank God for the things he has been Doing.]*

Raise Up Slowly—Move people incrementally toward leadership. Give them time to recover before handing them the responsibility of leadership. In the meantime, help them to serve in small ways: distributing communion at church, passing out songbooks, etc. Remember that disciples early in recovery are often not as healthy as they look.

Prioritize CR Meetings—CR must come first. Often, disciples early in recovery will want to miss a CR meeting to go and celebrate Mother's Day, a birthday, or whatever. Remind them that for years, however, those days that now seem so important never got in the way of their using. If someone is not willing to invest the same amount of time and effort in recovery as they were in getting high, they will never recover.

In discipling a former user, you must keep many things in mind. The payoff, though, is that you see more dramatic and rewarding changes in working with addicts than in perhaps any other ministry. God has a special place in his heart for those who are frequently passed over by the world and esteems those who have a similar attitude (Hebrews 6:10).

4

MIKE LEATHERWOOD

Disciples and Alcohol

To Drink or Not to Drink?

Since slavery to alcohol and other drugs affects a person physically, mentally, emotionally and spiritually, so recovery from drugs (alcohol included) must also include the whole person.

But how does this term "recovery" apply to the previously addicted disciple? Does it mean that once we receive the Holy Spirit we can control alcohol? That we can drink socially without negative consequences? Or does it mean, as Alcoholics Anonymous teaches, that once an alcoholic, always an alcoholic, that alcoholics have a disease that can only be arrested and never fully recovered from? Is recovery something to be achieved, or is it an ongoing process that we never attain? What does the Bible teach?

Sober Judgement

The Bible teaches that spiritual healing begins when one allows God's word to do its work. Hebrews 4:12-13 states:

> For the word of God is living and active. Sharper than any double-edged sword, it penetrates even to dividing soul and spirit, joints and marrow; it judges the thoughts and attitudes of the heart. Nothing in all creation is hidden from God's sight.

> Everything is uncovered and laid bare before the
> eyes of him to whom we must give account (He-
> brews 4:12-13).

The Bible is God's spiritual scalpel for cutting away sin and promoting spiritual recovery. As God's word works in our lives, we come to recognize that sins such as drunkenness have separated us from God and other people.

In cases where sin has progressed from abuse to slavery, we recognize that not only do we need God's forgiveness, we need his power to help us break free from this slavery to sin. Romans explains this slavery concept:

> We know that the law is spiritual; but I am
> unspiritual, sold as a slave to sin. For I have the
> desire to do what is good, but I cannot carry it out.
> For what I do is not the good I want to do; no, the
> evil I do not want to do—this I keep on doing. Now
> if I do what I do not want to do, it is no longer I
> who do it, but it is sin living in me that does it
> (Romans 7:14, 18b-19).

With God's help, we can turn from sin and have our lives washed completely clean of all its guilt and shame by the blood of Christ (Revelation 1:5). We are saved by his grace! In a very real sense we are no longer what we used to be. We are new creations (John 3:1-8; Colossians 3:1-14; 2 Corinthians 5:14-21). Paul states this very clearly:

> Do you not know that the wicked will not in-
> herit the kingdom of God? Do not be deceived:
> Neither the sexually immoral nor idolaters nor adul-
> terers nor male prostitutes nor homosexual offend-
> ers nor thieves nor the greedy nor drunkards nor
> slanderers nor swindlers will inherit the kingdom
> of God. And that is what some of you were. But
> you were washed, you were sanctified, you were

> justified in the name of the Lord Jesus Christ and
> by the Spirit of our God (1 Corinthians 6:9-11).

On the other hand, the Bible teaches that we still have a long way to go in order to be like Jesus (1 John 2:6). Colossians 1:28-29 reads:

> We proclaim him, admonishing and teaching everyone with all wisdom, so that we may present everyone perfect in Christ. To this end I labor, struggling with all his energy, which so powerfully works in me.

It is the relation of grace to the power of God's Spirit at work in us that enables us to continue this ongoing process of recovery from the ravages of sin. (See 2 Peter 1:5-11; 1 Corinthians 15:10; and 1 Corinthians 9:24-27.) Slavery to drugs and alcohol is no different. Even though we are washed clean and can say with confidence that we are not what we once were, we know that full recovery from the spiritual, emotional and mental damage that drugs have done to us and others will take some time. Recovery and spiritual growth are synonymous for the disciple.

I am grateful that in the kingdom we have repealed a man-made attitude of prohibition toward alcohol. We simply cannot make laws or enforce opinions where God has not spoken. It is also important to reiterate that the majority of people who use alcohol will do so with no ill effects. On the other hand, we need to realize that alcohol is a drug and one that Satan has used in the past to severely attack God's kingdom. Let's look at a brief history of the effects of alcohol in the Old Testament.

Alcohol Abuse in the Old Testament

The history of God's people in the Old Testament is quite checkered. If we look at the book of Judges, we see a disturbing pattern. First, God's people rebel against him. Second, God punishes them, and third, they are forgiven and restored, only to begin the cycle all over again. There are a number of reasons for Israel's fall: Pride, lust and a desire to be like the nations around them are but a few. One reason you've probably never considered before is the abuse of alcohol.

As early as Genesis, we see how alcohol began to take its toll on some of the heroes of the Bible. Noah, after his miraculous rescue from the flood, became drunk (Genesis 9:20-29). What should have been a time of tremendous unity and joy in Noah's family resulted in further action that caused one of Noah's sons to be cursed by God and the family to be torn apart. A few chapters later in Genesis 19, Lot's daughters, after being delivered from the fire and brimstone that destroyed Sodom and Gomorrah, proceeded to get their father drunk and have incestuous relations with him. Lot was so drunk that he had sex one night with his older daughter and then the next night repeated the sin with his youngest daughter. Both daughters became pregnant with their father's babies. Can you imagine the pain that the family had to endure for years to come because of Lot's drunkenness?

After the establishment of the twelve tribes, we are given considerable insight into the part that drunkenness and slavery (addiction) to alcohol played in the downfall of God's kingdom.

"Woe to those who rise early in the morning to run after their drinks, who stay up late at night till they are inflamed with wine" (Isaiah 5:11). One of the most common indications of an addiction to alcohol is drinking in the morning. These guys were drinking all day and into the night. They are focused on alcohol. Their slavery is obvious from the fact that they got up early "to run after their drinks." Later, Isaiah also writes,

> Woe to those who are heroes at drinking wine
>   and champions at mixing drinks,
> who acquit the guilty for a bribe,
>   but deny justice to the innocent (Isaiah 5:22).

These are judges, men in positions of responsibility, who are boastful about their drinking. The consequences of their behavior lead them to make unjust judgments and violate their vows of honesty and integrity in accepting bribes from the guilty.

Israel's destruction is directly tied to alcohol abuse in these powerful scriptures:

> Woe to that wreath, the pride of Ephraim's
>   drunkards,
>   to the fading flower, his glorious beauty,
> set on the head of a fertile valley—
>   to that city, the pride of those laid low by wine!
> See, the Lord has one who is powerful and strong.
>   Like a hailstorm and a destructive wind,
> like a driving rain and a flooding downpour,
>   he will throw it forcefully to the ground.
> That wreath, the pride of Ephraim's drunkards,
>   will be trampled underfoot.
> That fading flower, his glorious beauty,
>   set on the head of a fertile valley,
> will be like a fig ripe before harvest—
>   as soon as someone sees it and takes it in his
>   hand,
>   he swallows it.
> And these also stagger from wine
>   and reel from beer:
> Priests and prophets stagger from beer
>   and are befuddled with wine;
> they reel from beer,
>   they stagger when seeing visions,

> they stumble when rendering decisions.
> All the tables are covered with vomit
> and there is not a spot without filth
> (Isaiah 28:1-4, 7-8).

Slavery to alcohol was a leading cause in Israel's downfall. They had won the prize in drunkenness and the result was their pride being "laid low by wine." Again God gives the reason for their destruction: "that wreath, the pride of Ephraim's drunkards, will be trampled underfoot."

But it was the spiritual leaders who were the most responsible in the destruction of Israel. People generally imitate what they see in those who teach and have influence over them. Isaiah's words in verses 7-8 are tragic. Leaders had become addicted. It is sad to think that priests and prophets could get to this point. They continued to drink even though, in all likelihood, they must have felt horrible the next day, hung over, guilty and ashamed. Because we are often blind to the grossness of our sin, Isaiah graphically describes the scene. There was so much vomit that there was not a spot left that wasn't covered with its stench. Today drunkenness among priests and ministers has reached such a serious state in some churches that treatment centers have been set up exclusively for "impaired clergy."

Because most of us identify alcohol with celebrating and a good time, it is easy to overlook its potential for destruction. After all, many of us grew up with jokes about drunks and drunkenness. If even Bill Cosby can laugh about it, surely it can't be that bad! The problem is, though, that many of us never see the very real consequences for the alcoholic and his family.

Solomon's account of the drunkenness among God's people is graphically described in Proverbs:

Who has woe? Who has sorrow?
    Who has strife? Who has complaints?
    Who has needless bruises? Who has bloodshot
        eyes?
Those who linger over wine,
    who go to sample bowls of mixed wine.
Do not gaze at wine when it is red,
    when it sparkles in the cup,
    when it goes down smoothly!
In the end it bites like a snake
    and poisons like a viper.
Your eyes will see strange sights
    and your mind imagine confusing things.
You will be like one sleeping on the high seas,
    lying on top of the rigging.
"They hit me," you will say, "but I'm not hurt!
    They beat me, but I don't feel it!
When will I wake up
    so I can find another drink?"
        (Proverbs 23:29-35).

Drinking Among Disciples

My own experience with alcohol and other drugs began in my early teens. A doctor prescribed for me what in 1964 was thought to be a relatively harmless drug, Valium. I took Valium for mild attacks of nervousness off and on for several years. As I got older and Valium became increasingly more difficult to get, I discovered that alcohol produced the same feeling and did not require a prescription.

My self-medication went on for twelve years. A glass of wine turned into a bottle of wine or a six-pack of beer. I would, at times, combine alcohol with Valium, a potentially lethal combination. I always drank for the effect. Not that I didn't like the taste of alcohol: I did, but *how* I drank was very different from the way that most people drink. You see, I could not identify with the social drinker who was comfortable with a glass of wine or a beer. I never drank that way unless I was trying to prove to myself or to someone else that I could maintain control.

If someone offered me a glass of wine, my response would be to decline because, honestly, a glass of wine would just serve to frustrate me. "A" glass is not what I would really want, so I would prefer to just not drink at all.

Before my recovery I, at times, fooled myself into thinking that I could drink one or two and was successful for a short time. However, after a period of proving to myself that I was still in control, I would inevitably and unpredictably have another drunken episode. I could not predict when it would happen, and I still cannot. This is what it means to lose control, to be powerless.

I am very concerned today with all of us, both in and out of leadership, who have experienced similar situations either before or after becoming a disciple and are still attempting to drink. I have had Christians in church leadership tell me that they really felt there were times when they drank too much and they were going to quit, only to see or hear about them drinking again.

Recently, I heard about several brothers who were having beers at a bachelor party. One brother drank four beers and another brother who is in the full-time ministry had a flask filled with whiskey. When one of the brothers confronted him about it he simply replied that his wife had bought it for him.

Not too long ago, I asked several disciples in another ministry when they had gotten high or intoxicated last. Out of ten people in the group, eight had quit drinking when they became disciples, but because liquor was served at so many church-related functions, their last high, buzz, or whatever you want to call a period of intoxication, was at a function sponsored by disciples. Some of these same disciples were laughing about a brother who had too much to drink at a disciple's wedding. I know a case where a young Christian saw leaders drink, and even had leaders encourage him to drink, only to fall tragically back into several bouts of drunkenness. Such a cavalier attitude toward alcohol should alarm those of us in positions of leadership.

My biggest concerns are the following: (1) leaders who have experienced recent periods of intoxication and continue to drink, and (2) the effect that leaders drinking and the proliferation of alcohol at disciples' functions is going to have on those who have a history of slavery to drugs and alcohol. If we learn anything from Israel's history, we need to learn to respect the power of alcohol or any mood-altering substance to enslave those of us who are leaders, as well as those we lead.

There are four reasons why I believe a disciple who has been enslaved to alcohol or other drugs should not attempt to use alcohol or other mood-altering drugs at all. In 2 Corinthians 7:10-11 Paul states,

> Godly sorrow brings repentance that leads to salvation and leaves no regret, but worldly sorrow brings death. See what this godly sorrow has produced in you: what earnestness, what eagerness to clear yourselves, what indignation, what alarm, what longing, what concern, what readiness to see justice done. At every point you have proved yourselves to be innocent in this matter.

It is obvious from this passage that our sorrow for what we have done to God, others and ourselves as a result of substance abuse should motivate us to stay as far away from this sin as possible. While I certainly recognize that a glass of wine or a beer is not inherently sinful, it seems foolish to me that we who have been addicted should not renounce it completely. Some of us understood this clearly when we were first baptized, but for some reason it has become fuzzy again.

We have no problem applying this principle with regard to other sins. We know that Satan can use areas in which we've been particularly vulnerable in the past to lure us back into sin. We know that we must absolutely avoid certain people, places and things. Let's not lower our guard simply because we have been disciples a few months or years.

Second, experience in the CR ministry has allowed me to see many disciples who were previously addicted attempt to drink socially. Some never made it back.

Third, numerous studies in recent years show a physical component to addiction. There are some who appear to have either been born with an altered brain chemistry, or have developed this condition as a result of continued abuse. When these people attempt to use alcohol or other mood-altering substances, a craving is triggered which often results in drunkenness.[1] For some disciples in recovery, attempts to drink may not necessarily result in an episode of drunkenness. After all, we know that drunkenness is a sin. Yet, what we may find is that a glass of wine or a beer will leave us wanting more. What follows may be a period of irritability, moodiness or general discontent. We are able to fight the temptation of drunkenness, but not the negative emotions associated with this desire. This condition has been referred to as being a "dry drunk." You are not getting drunk, but you are miserable either not using or attempting to use in moderation. Such periods of discomfort associated with the use of alcohol are evidence of a life that is not surrendered. This is one of the key issues addressed in our chemical recovery groups. The goal of recovery is to be at peace not using drugs.

The fourth and final reason why I believe that a person with a background of chemical addiction should not attempt to use alcohol or other mood-altering substances is that there are some things that God permits us to do that under some circumstances, we should not do.

> "Everything is permissible"—but not everything is beneficial. "Everything is permissible"—but not everything is constructive. Nobody should seek his own good, but the good of others (1 Corinthians 10:23-24).

Even though drinking is certainly permitted, those of us who have been previously addicted need to say no because the result will probably not be beneficial for us or for the kingdom.

No Stumbling Blocks

This is probably a good place to talk about responsible drinking in the kingdom. The fact is that some of us need to grow in our sensitivity to others when it comes to exercising our freedom to drink.

A couple of years ago I was asked to do a wedding for some disciples. We had the usual rehearsal and then dinner. I expected at dinner that people would have a glass of wine or a toast. I am usually pretty comfortable being in this situation because I just keep telling myself that it won't last long and it is okay for them, etc. The problem came when the wine continued to be served throughout the meal and afterwards. I did not notice anyone getting drunk, but I felt very uncomfortable because I did not want to leave, yet I also did not want to sit and smell alcohol throughout dinner. I felt a little angry and hurt that one of my close friends who knew my background would be so inconsiderate. We talked afterward, and he said that it just did not occur to him that it would be a problem. I am sure that was true. I knew that he loved me and would not do anything to intentionally hurt me, but the fact remains that not developing a sensitivity in this area can have disastrous consequences.

A few months ago I heard about a birthday party that had been planned for one of the women who had graduated from CR. The organizers had planned to serve wine at the party when someone realized that it would probably be inappropriate. They had just not thought it through. We have had people in the CR groups talk about how they struggled baby-sitting for leaders because there was a lot of wine and beer around, and they were there alone with it. I don't want to ever use my conscience or anyone else's to restrict what God has allowed, but we must never allow our freedom to cause someone to fall back into sin. As Paul states so clearly:

> Let us therefore make every effort to do what leads to peace and to mutual edification. Do not destroy the work of God for the sake of food. All food is clean, but it is wrong for a man to eat anything that causes someone else to stumble. It is better not to eat meat or drink wine or to do anything else that will cause your brother to fall (Romans 14:19-21).

> Be careful, however, that the exercise of your freedom does not become a stumbling block to the weak (1 Corinthians 8:9).

Not everyone who has abused alcohol or even experienced negative consequences in the past has developed a slavery or addiction. While I would certainly encourage such people that the safest course is not to use at all, there are some who seem to have abused alcohol in the past without lasting effects. I have been with disciples who have a background of drug abuse but who seem to be able to use without episodes of drunkenness or negative emotions related to attempting to use in moderation. If you can use alcohol in moderation even though you have abused alcohol or other drugs in the past, then you may be immune. However, it is extremely important to be honest with yourself. So much is really at stake. If you attempt to use in moderation and you are truly addicted, time will ultimately tell.

5

MIKE LEATHERWOOD

No More Playing God

The Serenity to Accept the Things I Cannot Change

Nothing is more frustrating than trying to help someone we cannot help. Even when it's obvious that we are having no effect, there is a part of us that just insists on trying to figure people out: "Surely there is something else I could say," we tell ourselves. "Perhaps if I just did...." Such frustration is typical of what we feel when we make efforts to help those with substance abuse problems.

Good Intentions

In 1980 in Louisville, Kentucky, Brenda and I, along with Sonny and Carolyn Sessions, Don and Alice Peden and two other couples began a ministry in the downtown area. The old part of the city which surrounds the university was experiencing a period of drastic change. Neighborhoods long deteriorated by drugs and poverty were beginning to improve as young professionals moved into the area. They bought and refurbished many Victorian homes lining Third, Fourth, Fifth and Sixth Streets. While we initiated and built relationships with all types of people during our first two years in Louisville, the majority of people with whom we ministered to had alcohol and drug backgrounds.

The problems these people experienced were overwhelming. Financial, marital, legal, emotional and substance abuse problems inundated their lives and consequently, spilled over into ours. We helped to pay their bills, counseled their marriages, went to court with them, poured out their alcohol, threw away their drugs, but the problems only grew. Our many attempts to meet their needs invariably ended in failure.

While there were a number of exciting things happening in the ministry, we were frustrated by too many situations in which what we did only seemed to make things worse. Instead of us helping to heal people's lives we seemed to be helping them get sicker. We prayed to God for wisdom and for help, and he amazingly worked through two unfortunate situations in answering our prayers.

First was the death of a young woman my wife had studied with and baptized. She had left the church, returned to drugs and prostitution and was eventually found murdered. At the funeral, I remember feeling sad, but also angry and stupid since we had watched her get worse in spite of all our efforts.

A few weeks after the funeral, an extremely bright freshman at the University of Louisville, with whom I had been studying the Bible, called me and said that he needed some help. I drove over to his house and found him in his mother's basement lying on a mattress. Beside him were two empty bottles of liquid shoe polish and a large empty bottle of Scope mouthwash. He had poured the shoe polish through slices of bread in order to strain out the dye and then drank the polish and the mouthwash to get high.

I rushed him to the hospital. Needless to say he was sick for several days and then was sent to a drug treatment center. When I visited him, several of the counselors seemed surprised that a minister would take a serious interest in this young man's recovery. Impressed, they invited me to attend some lectures on chemical recovery at the treatment center.

Brenda and I both began attending the sessions and in a matter of weeks, God helped us see a fundamental principle which has been one of the keys to the success we've experienced with addicts here in New York.

Accepting Our Limitations

The principle is that we are "not God."[1] Now that may not seem revolutionary to you, but for many of us it is, practically speaking. Some of us are so frustrated or guilt-ridden over a mistake we have made, we give up trying to work with this "high risk" group of people. I want to suggest that if you are fed up, angry or guilty, it is because you have not accepted your own limitations.

One morning, after a long night of pouring out liquor, staying up with a guy, then dropping by the next morning to make sure that he made it to his job interview, I visited one of my friends, a counselor at a treatment center. Although I was tired and feeling concerned about the alcoholic's ability to stay sober that day, overall I felt quite noble about how I had helped. As I talked to my friend about the previous night, he abruptly asked me, "When do you intend to stop playing God and get off your white horse?" I was shocked and offended. After all, I was doing what Jesus would do. Or was I? I knew something was wrong. His comment rattled me but also challenged me to go back and look at how Jesus ministered to people.

It is amazing to see that each individual Jesus encountered was at a different place spiritually. Some needed a greater faith, some needed to repent, but in each encounter, Jesus never seemed frustrated or anxious, whatever the outcome.

One of the best illustrations of this is Jesus' interaction with the rich young man in Mark 10:17-31. Isn't it interesting that the Bible records how Jesus looked at him and loved him before telling him to go sell everything and give the money to the poor? The man went away sad because he didn't have enough faith to trust God and surrender it all.

How would you feel after a reaction like the rich young man's? Would you feel fearful, guilty or angry because he didn't come around? Would you have second-guessed yourself or have been tempted to run after him and maybe eased up on God's standard a bit? Why is it that many of us have to control the outcome or we feel like failures? I believe that as well-meaning as we might be, our need to control is sinful. The Bible sometimes calls it pride, other times a lack of faith, but in a sense, we are playing God. Instead of accepting our limitations and being at peace about a situation, our pride breeds insecurity, anxiety and unhappiness in us.

I don't believe that Jesus was ever glib about people turning away. You cannot love people without feeling sad for them when they reject the help God offers. But a normal degree of sadness is very different from the intense discouragement some of us feel when we cannot get someone to do what we think they ought to do. In the case of the rich young man, Jesus goes on to explain to his disciples that he wasn't shocked or discouraged by the man's response (Mark 10:23-25). As a matter of fact, Jesus thought that it was typical for a rich man to fail to come into the kingdom. Although I am sure Jesus was disappointed, he was at peace doing what he had been sent to do, that is, the will of his Father.

Are you okay with doing what you have been sent to say and do? Or is your peace dependent on others' response to you? If so, you are being robbed of the joy and peace Jesus intended you to experience by your pride and lack of faith. The deceptive thing is that most of us do not detect these sins because they are so hidden in our concern for people. Sometimes it takes hitting bottom (as Brenda and I did in Louisville) before we can begin to really see our own sin.

Paul, in confronting the pride in the Corinthian church, made it clear that the solution is to stop playing God. We plant and water, but it is God who makes things grow. The whole issue comes down to surrendering our pride and its consequent fear. We need to let go and let God be God. How refreshing! Surely taking the message of redemption to the whole world is enough to keep us busy.

Wholeheartedly embracing these principles will revolutionize our effectiveness in working with the drug addict. There are at least three ways this concept applies to our working with those who abuse mood-altering substances.

First, we need to realize that most of the problems in the life of an alcoholic or drug addict are a direct result of one fundamental problem: the continued abuse of alcohol and other drugs. If we attempt to "help" them with every other problem but do not address alcohol or drug abuse as the primary problem, we will inevitably watch them get sicker and sicker.[2]

Second, we must get okay, and I mean really okay, with the fact that we can only help those people who are open to our help. In the Parable of the Prodigal Son (Luke 15:11-20), I'm sure that the father wanted very much to go and find his son, but he knew that the son had to hit bottom and come back totally humbled. It took a famine, moral and spiritual bankruptcy, and finally the desperation of "no one giving him anything" (v. 16) to bring him to his senses.

Sometimes the most loving and most difficult thing we can do is wait. Those of us who been through this know that "doing nothing" can be one of the hardest things that we will ever do. Waiting for God to work and for people to be humbled opens the door for us to plant and water with joy and enthusiasm.

Third, we must accept that not everyone we meet has hit his bottom. We simply cannot tell by listening or even by looking at him. Again, the rich young man sounded broken and looked humble as he fell on his knees before the Lord, but he wasn't. As soon as Jesus told him what he needed to do, he split.

We need to stop believing what people say, or even how they appear. We need to start paying attention to what they do. We should pull for someone and want to believe the best, but when that keeps us from hearing the truth of his actions, then we are not only frustrating ourselves—we are failing to really love him the way that Jesus did. We are, in effect, "loving him to death." Jesus listened to what the young man *did*. He let him go without guilt or fear. He was at peace because he knew he had done all he could. Surely, none of us is so arrogant as to think that we could have done more in that situation than Jesus did. Yet, don't we essentially do this when we second-guess him by our faithless pride, evidenced by our frustration when working with the alcoholic or drug addict?

"But he or she sounded so sincere! They seemed so eager and broken. How can I tell who is genuine and who isn't?" Your ability to really help the addict will lie in his willingness to do what you ask him to do. If, when you propose solutions, he argues, or seems agreeable but wants to change your plan ever so slightly, beware. The person truly broken by his addiction will be willing to go to any lengths to do precisely what you ask him. What it takes for someone to hit bottom varies with the individual, but the results are always the same: surrender (Luke 15:17-20).

Tough Love

Let me give you an example of a difficult situation we faced in one of our groups. Recently a young man who had been baptized was scheduled to read his journal, that is, a personal history of his addiction, in one of our CR groups. The CR group leader asked me to sit in on the group since the guy had been a little defensive in previous meetings.

The journal has a definite format. People are told to write down precisely: (1) what they used (that is, the type of drug and how much), (2) what happened when they used (that is, the consequences), and (3) how they felt after these consequences. They are to begin with the first time they used and write down every episode of abuse they can remember, until they reach the last episode. Of course, people won't remember everything, but they need to take great pains and make great efforts to write down everything they do remember, especially how they felt.

As this young man began reading, he first explained why he had changed the format of the journal. He said that he was having trouble expressing his heart and emotions, and that he knew we (the group) would not want his genuine desire to be open to be restricted by the structure of the journal.

I watched as every brother in the group was gradually pulled into his manipulation. It was obvious that this kid was really good because there were some very perceptive guys in the group. Before he started to read from his actual journal, I stopped him and asked him if he realized what he had done. He seemed a little puzzled and said no. I told him that he had done exactly what he wanted to do, and that this type of unwillingness to follow directions was going to make it virtually impossible for him to recover. I tried to explain that no one could help him until he got humble, and I told him that he would need to do the journal over again. He promptly got up, started yelling and stomped out, slamming the door behind him. The brothers were shocked. What if he went out and used? I explained to them that his actions, both in failing to follow directions with the journal and in leaving, indicated an attitude which would inevitably result in relapsing.

I wish that I could tell you that there is a happy ending to the story. As yet there is not. Notice, I said "as yet." Sometimes it takes just this kind of response to bring someone to God. I wanted to share this story because I believe many would relate to the group. We would have been uncomfortable with the confrontation and most likely fearful and guilty about the outcome. "What if he goes out and gets high, and something happens?"

How do you think Jesus would have felt if the rich young man had left and been killed that evening? Sad? Yes, but not guilty. You see, we need to learn how to really love those who are addicted. They need our kindness, our compassion and the truth about what it will take to recover. They need us to love them enough to tell them the truth and stop allowing them to destroy themselves and others by manipulation.

We will see people and wonder how in the world they could be so obstinate in changing. They've been through so much, surely they've had enough! We need to humbly remember that we all have to hit bottom at some time, but unfortunately some will have to die and face God before their knees will bow (Philippians 2:10). I am convinced that successfully winning and discipling those addicted to alcohol and other drugs is going to require pouring our lives into the people whose hearts God has prepared for us, and prayerfully and peacefully waiting on many who need more time to be humbled by God.[3]

6

MIKE LEATHERWOOD

Intervention

The Courage to Change the Things I Can

Although we must learn to accept our limitations when helping the chemically dependent, this doesn't mean we can do nothing. There are things we can change to help the addict, if we ask God to give us the courage to do so. Intervention is all about learning what we can constructively do in the life of the addict to help him come to a point of surrender.

Daunting Prospect

This idea, for someone closely bound up in the life of an alcoholic or drug addict, can be a daunting prospect. You may still be too fearful or guilty to act. Two things may have to happen before you decide. First, you must be convinced that the right way to act toward the chemically dependent person in your life is determined by the truth, not by how you feel. Focusing on God's principles in this book and developing a soberness about what is going on in your life will help you overcome your feelings of guilt and fear and gain a conviction which will move you to act. Second, the pain in your life may have to intensify until you realize your powerlessness over the addict. Then you can actually start helping him hit bottom instead of trying to save him from it.

There is a prayer which is used frequently in recovery circles known as the "Serenity Prayer." It states:

> God grant me the serenity to accept
> the things I cannot change,
> the courage to change the things I can,
> and the wisdom to know the difference.

Intervention is about having the courage to change the things you can. It is a decision to intervene in the life of the addict in such a way as to help him: (1) begin to receive the painful consequences related to using drugs, (2) connect the physical, emotional, and spiritual pain he is experiencing with his drug use, and (3) ask for help.

Intervening is not about trying to control, get even or inflict pain. It is an effort to break out of the rescuer-victim-persecutor cycle by learning to help instead of hurt. Every addict has to hit bottom before they are humble enough to ask for help. Intervention is a serious attempt to help raise the addict's bottom in the hope of preventing a lower bottom, or death.[1]

Informal Intervention

What are some practical things we might do to step in and encourage our friend or relative to get the help they need so desperately? There are two types of intervention: formal and informal. Since informal interventions are usually attempted before the more formal type, let's take a look at these first:

The husband, a practicing alcoholic, is attempting to shave and get ready for work after a night of serious drinking. Hung over, he is in the process of telling himself for the one-hundredth time that something has to change, when his wife passes the bathroom door. She cheerfully calls out as she heads for work that she'll be late coming home because she is going to an Al Anon Meeting (for those who live with addicts).

"A what?" he yells back at her from the bathroom. "Why in the world are you going to one of those stupid meetings for? You don't even drink."

"Yes, I know, honey," she says in a calm voice. "I'm going for me so I can learn how to live with your drinking. See you tonight! There's a frozen dinner in the freezer. Love ya!"

Intervention! I think she got his attention. She didn't harp or cajole. She didn't pour out his liquor. She just decided to control the only person she could: herself. Notice she didn't say she was going to get help for him, but for herself: "I'm going for me."

But what if this intervention doesn't work? If he continues to drink, doesn't that mean it failed? No. Granted, he is not in treatment yet, but she is feeling better. As she continues to improve emotionally, mentally and spiritually, his chances of getting help continue to improve as well.

One evening he stumbles home after happy hour and notices a letter on the table from an attorney. The letter states simply that his wife is seeking legal counsel about the future of their marriage. There is no threat. The lawyer gives no details of the discussion, just that it occurred out of concern for the marriage. Now, this gets his undivided attention! He is initially shaken, but collects himself and then gets angry: "I can't believe she would do that to me! How dare she see a lawyer without talking to me!" As he storms into the kitchen, she first lets him vent and then calmly reminds him that she has discussed her inability to live under these conditions innumerable times. He should not be surprised. He responds by getting another drink.

The next morning he "comes to," feeling sick and tired after his usual night of drinking. He tells himself for the hundred-and-first time, "I have to do something." He remembers the letter and another night alone with a frozen dinner while his wife goes off to her meeting. He remembers her mentioning an AA meeting across the hall from her meeting. "Perhaps tonight I'll go," he tells himself.

These examples are not necessarily what you should do specifically, but are used to stimulate your thinking. Be thoughtful, creative, and get advice in deciding how best to intervene and help your practicing substance abuser hit bottom. Chapters 8 and 9 on codependency should help you with practical ways to intervene. Remember, the goal is to get the alcoholic or drug addict to *do* something, not to just agree to or talk about doing something. Please don't forget that the addict is powerless over mood-altering drugs and will not recover without the help of God and others. Don't make the common mistake of listening to good intentions. Be consistent, and insist on treatment. The chilling reality is that there are only are only three alternatives for the addict: death, insanity or recovery.

Formal Intervention

Formal intervention is a great deal more structured. There are treatment centers in your area or certified counselors who can help you in designing and implementing this plan, but the principles are as follows.

First of all, you will need to identify "significant others" in the addict's life. These are people who have some degree of influence or leverage in his or her life. They may include, but are not limited to, spouses, children, parents, boss, family doctors or best friends. Ask each of them to meet together, out of concern for their friend or family member. Usually a trained counselor will convene the meeting, outline the format and facilitate the intervention.

Everyone is told that the goal of their being together is to rehearse a plan which hopefully will motivate their friend or loved one to seek help for their addiction. The concerned persons are told that the addict will be persuaded to come to a meeting, but will be unaware of the true nature of the meeting until he arrives. Upon walking in, he will be asked to sit and listen to the concerns that the others have for him. Somewhat shaken, he will probably agree to stay and hear everyone out. If not, be prepared for the possibility that the meeting may not even happen. Some addicts may walk in, turn around and walk out the door. Most will stay, however, out of respect for the people in the group.

At this point each person is instructed to express his or her concern. First, reinforce your love for them. Second, remind them of a specific drinking episode and describe what happened. Third, tell them how you felt. It is important to say how you felt not how they made you feel. Use the words, "I felt hurt," not "You made me feel angry." Most of us are hurt before we get angry and besides, this is a time for intervention, not ventilation. Fourth, ask them to get help. Intervention might go something like this.

1. *John, I love you.*
2. *Last week you were drinking and you screamed at our daughter.*
3. *I felt hurt and afraid of you.*
4. *Please, will you go to an AA meeting?*

Start with the most influential person, place the less influential in the middle and end with another person very important to the addict. You may repeat this rotation two or three times. In many cases this will be enough to persuade the person to go for help. If the addict agrees to get treatment, have a treatment center ready for them immediately. Have a bag packed, transportation planned and arrangements made with his employer. If it is impossible to take a leave of absence without his being fired, then remember that recovery must take precedence over a job. He can get another job, but he cannot get another life. Most companies have employee assistance programs or a human resource representative who will be eager to work with you in order to keep a valuable or well-trained employee.

If the first phase of the intervention is unsuccessful and the addict is still refusing to get help, then you will have to implement phase two. At this point, each concerned person intervenes to help get the addict into treatment through "raising his bottom." Each person addresses the addict by first reaffirming his or her love, and then by stating the consequence of the addict's refusal to get help.

> *John, "I love you and until you get some help, you will have to:*
> *...move out of the house" (spouse).*
> *...not come to visit the grandchildren" (daughter).*
> *...see another doctor" (family physician).*
> *...get another job" (boss).*

You can see how effective this can be. Very few people are able to withstand such leverage. The dangerous thing is that it only takes one key person in the group to get cold feet in order for the entire intervention to fail. Each person must be willing to state his or her conviction and then be prepared to follow through regardless of the consequences. The effectiveness of the intervention rests on the united effort of everyone in the group. The more painful the consequences, the better the addict's chances are of choosing to get help. Remember that pain is what humbles a person and ultimately moves him to seek help. Every "significant other" in the group must be thoroughly convinced that if the practicing alcoholic or drug addict does not get help there are now only two alternatives for him: insanity or death.

But does forcing someone into treatment work? Yes! Everyone is, in effect, forced into treatment by the consequences of their drug use. Although addicts can be forced to seek treatment because of legal, health or family problems, it usually takes a combination of these painful circumstances converging on them before they seek help.

Keep in mind that there are no guarantees. We personally have to get better whether the alcoholic does or not. All we can do is have the courage to change the things we can and then ask God for the serenity to accept the things we cannot.

7

MIKE LEATHERWOOD

Approaches to Treatment

The Wisdom to Know the Difference

There are several reasons to familiarize ourselves with the various types of substance abuse treatment. First, we cannot work effectively with addicts unless we know what type of treatment, if any, they have received. It is also helpful to know if they completed any program and how long they remained drug free afterwards. Second, even when you have a CR ministry in your church, it may be necessary for you to refer a person into an alcohol- or drug-treatment center at some point. Making an appropriate referral will require a thorough knowledge of what is available and appropriate. Third, if your church does not have a chemical recovery ministry, it may be helpful to refer a person who is very early in his recovery into some form of treatment. Understanding the treatments available will help you assess the seriousness of the problem and his level of motivation to recover. It will also help you provide him with help in staying sober before and after his conversion. Participation in some type of treatment may be necessary to establish a period of continuous sobriety essential to a person's conversion.

AA and Other Twelve-Step Programs

Alcoholics Anonymous has been by far the most effective treatment program for alcoholics. Its tenets are stated in the form of twelve steps which are listed and explained in a basic text named simply *Alcoholics Anonymous* or, by AA adherents, "The Big Book."[1] Essential to AA's "suggested" plan of recovery are:

1. An admission that one is powerless over alcohol.
2. Acknowledgment of the need for a higher power.
3. Participation in a fellowship made up of other alcoholics.
4. A conviction that abstinence is essential to recovery.
5. A commitment to take it "one day at a time."

As you interact with people in AA you will find a varied response to the Bible. The overall attitude will be one of suspicion. This reaction can be better understood if we realize that most AA members have probably not had good experiences with "organized" religion. Old-timers in AA may have seen religious people encourage those early in recovery not to attend AA, only to watch them relapse into drinking and, in some cases, die. They view Christianity as having utterly failed the alcoholic, and Christians as a real threat, discouraging the recovering alcoholic from the only thing they know that works. If you are patient and take the time to convince people in AA of your genuine love and concern, some will eventually see how God has used AA as a stepping stone into a saving relationship with him.

Narcotics Anonymous (NA), like AA, is a twelve-step program with a spiritual component (Higher Power). It was formed in the 1970s because many in AA were uncomfortable with drug addicts attending their meetings. Since that time there have been a proliferation of twelve-step programs, including Gamblers Anonymous, Overeaters Anonymous, and Emotions Anonymous.

Attending AA or NA meetings can be very helpful, especially if there is no chemical recovery ministry in your church. A few precautions should be taken, though. First, make sure that a more mature Christian goes with a younger Christian in order to be able to spiritually filter the advice given in the meeting. Second, be careful that AA meetings do not take precedence over church services. Third, do not let young Christians get a sponsor in AA (or NA). Sponsors are older AA members that serve as "discipling partners" in AA. While having a sponsor is an extremely important part of the AA program, disciples should not have AA sponsors who are not disciples because they will inevitably give advice that will directly conflict with God's word.

People who attend AA refer to it as a "fellowship."[2] They consider attendance at AA meetings just as critical to sobriety as we regard attendance at our fellowship essential to remaining faithful to God. Their experience has taught them that people who stop coming to meetings will eventually get drunk.

Sometimes people who have been a part of AA for many years begin coming to church and studying the Bible. We need to understand that for them, putting the church first may require a great deal of faith. AA has saved their life and they consider this "fellowship" critical to their ability to stay sober and therefore alive. They often view putting the church first as tantamount to putting their recovery second, which is a very frightening thought. We need to patiently reassure them that putting the kingdom first is an investment in their recovery and not a threat to it, that God has always had a plan of recovery through the church and that they have nothing to fear.

You may find some young Christians who feel the need to continue to attend AA meetings after their baptism. They may feel more secure in their sobriety by attending meetings or they may have friends that they want to reach out to. I would not discourage it as long they are willing to follow the guidelines above. What I have shared with people in this situation is that they will probably find themselves outgrowing AA and their need for it. This approach allows people time to overcome their fears of leaving AA without compromising their biblical convictions.

For information about an AA or NA meeting locally, look up Alcoholics Anonymous in the phone book. You can get a list of all the AA and NA meetings in your area at any local meeting. I would encourage you to get *Alcoholics Anonymous*, AA's basic handbook, and read it. There is a lot of very helpful information and tools for staying sober. Pay special attention to Chapter Five, "How it Works." Bear in mind that some meetings are open to people who are not alcoholics, and others are not. The meetings list will have a code as follows:

> CD - Closed Discussion
> OD - Open Discussion
> OS - Open Speaker
> CS - Closed Speaker

Discussion meetings may cover a topic related to recovery, one of the Twelve Steps, or a portion of the text of *Alcoholics Anonymous*. Speaker meetings consist of a recovering alcoholic telling his or her story. Since you will find some meetings better than others, I would recommend that you attend a variety of meetings and locations. (Since AA meetings are ironically filled with nicotine addicts, you might want to attend a nonsmoking meeting.) Disciples may find meetings with speakers of special value. Relating emotionally to someone's story will help you get in touch with, as they say in AA, "what it was like, what happened and what it is like now." Connecting pain with addiction will cause you to leave with a renewed sense of surrender and acceptance. (AA and NA meetings are designed to help the addict be at peace and comfortable with not using, one day at a time.)

Detoxification

Another type of treatment is detox centers. These are usually affiliated with a hospital or independent drug-treatment program and provide a period of drying out, that is, physically detoxifying from drugs. The length of stay depends on the type of drug and the severity of the addiction. Detoxification may last from three days to two weeks. These centers generally provide a clean, safe environment in which to physically withdraw from the effects of drugs or alcohol.

Most detox centers that are medically oriented provide sedatives which minimize the effects of withdrawal, while others are totally drug free. Since detoxing can be life threatening, the center is usually staffed with a doctor and a registered nurse. Some detox centers are nonmedical and use emergency services only in case of a life-threatening situation.

Heroin addicts are often only partially detoxified and placed on methadone, a synthetic opiate. Methadone was developed by the criminal justice system in order to control the increased use of heroin and to cut down on the crime associated with heroin use. People placed on methadone are usually "maintained," or kept on methadone, for years. (In my opinion, methadone maintenance is not a form of treatment, but a legal way for people to continue to get high. People should be detoxified from methadone before they are baptized, although withdrawal is often more difficult than withdrawal from heroin.) After physically detoxing, some addicts can return and continue their spiritual, emotional and mental recovery through the church. Others may need further treatment in an inpatient or intensive outpatient setting.

Outpatient Counseling

The third approach to treatment is outpatient counseling. Because inpatient, or residential, treatment is so expensive, many insurance companies today are more inclined to pay for an outpatient program. These programs vary a great deal, from a one-hour appointment one time a week to a very intensive, five-day-a-week, 9:00 A.M.-5:00 P.M. regimen. Some programs have different phases, moving from very intense to less intense as people progress in their recovery. Random urine tests to check for drug use are often required to help keep the addict honest. The benefits of outpatient programs are: (1) They are less expensive; (2) They often allow a person to keep his job; (3) They are less disruptive to the family. The major liability is that a person can easily manipulate programs which allow more flexibility and require less accountability than inpatient programs.

Residential Programs

The fourth type of treatment is the residential or inpatient program. These centers are useful when outpatient programs have failed or for people who feel the need to go directly into a more restrictive program due to the severity of their addiction. Many people choose this approach to treatment first because the more time they invest in treatment, the better their chances of staying sober.

Traditional Inpatient Treatment

Some inpatient programs are freestanding, others are part of a multipurpose hospital. Most require a three to five-day stay in a detox unit followed by twenty to twenty-five days in a residential setting. These three weeks in residence are traditionally made up of drug education, small group interaction and several AA meetings a week. Inpatient programs may vary in duration depending on insurance coverage. Some long-term inpatient treatment programs (six months to one year) may be supplemented by local, state or federal funding.

Upon completion, traditional AA-based inpatient treatment programs encourage participation in a weekly outpatient group for two years and AA meetings several times a week as a part of an aftercare plan. Some treatment programs recommend ninety AA meetings in the first ninety days out of treatment.

Because some people cannot, or for various reasons should not, return home after completing their inpatient treatment, halfway houses provide a low-cost, drug-free environment for further recovery during the first several months.

Inpatient Psychiatric Treatment

Great care should be taken when referring people for inpatient treatment. Programs affiliated with psychiatric hospitals will have a mental health orientation. People referred to these facilities will most often be given a psychiatric diagnosis other than substance abuse. Many times addicts are placed on other types of drugs and treated with psychotherapy instead of being completely detoxified and treated for recovery from drugs and alcohol. Since the mental health community is dominated by psychiatrists, it should not surprise us that treatment begins with drugs, followed by an effort to help the addict "understand" why he uses. It is often wrongly assumed that if a person knows why he uses, then he will somehow be empowered to stop his self-destructive drug use. In addition, most mental health treatment has little or no emphasis on the spiritual aspect of recovery.[3]

Having said that, it is important to mention that some people will have what is known as a "dual diagnosis," meaning they have both a substance abuse problem and some form of mental illness which may require medication. This can be a difficult situation if the prescribed drug is one which the addict has abused in the past. This is one reason for establishing a working relationship with a good supportive psychiatrist when referring someone for inpatient care. Utilizing a mental health facility will be essential in some situations, and often medications prescribed by a psychiatrist are given to prevent life-threatening episodes. We should never encourage anyone to discontinue their medication, even if we believe it may be interfering with their recovery.

Working as part of the treatment team with doctors or counselors in an inpatient or even an outpatient setting is both possible and necessary. It is important that the person being referred fills out a release of information form with your name listed as the person with whom the doctor or counselor may discuss the patient's progress. This ensures that you will be able to work together with his primary counselor and assist in planning an appropriate aftercare. It is important that you demonstrate to the other members of the treatment team your genuine interest in the patient's welfare and your desire to work together with them.

Therapeutic Community

The last type of formal inpatient program is what has been referred to as a Therapeutic Community, or TC. In a TC, a community of recovering addicts is the primary source of healing. TCs were designed in the late '50s and early '60s to address behavior related to narcotic addiction. Most people referred to these programs were probated through the courts in lieu of incarceration and the length of stay was usually one to two years. The treatment focused on altering drug-related behavior through intense behavior modification and was calculated to produce abstinence from narcotics. TCs, in their original format, failed for at least three reasons:

1. Abstinence from all drugs (including alcohol) was never the goal.
2. Powerlessness over mood-altering substances was never addressed.
3. A humanistic assumption was made that behavior modification could produce a person who would stay clean.

As a result of their failures, most TCs have modified their approach and now combine various types of therapy with a strong AA component. Long-term programs of this nature should be used only in extreme cases.

Overall, inpatient treatment can be very expensive, but a good insurance policy will usually cover the costs of a twenty-eight-day program. Some treatment centers will accept Medicaid and will even admit clients and assist them in obtaining Medicaid if they have not previously qualified. A few treatment programs help those who have zero resources and may only charge on a sliding scale, meaning that the truly indigent are totally free. I would encourage you or someone in your church to familiarize yourself with the types of treatment and methods of payment available in your community. Building a relationship with the director of one or more programs may very well insure that a bed will be available when you need it. Otherwise, you might have to wait several days to get someone into treatment.

Shelters and Halfway Houses

An alternative to inpatient treatment may be a shelter. Most cities provide shelters for men, women and even families. Although these shelters provide little or no treatment, they can be a valuable resource. Shelters vary a great deal in terms of cleanliness, safety and rules of admission. They are usually free, although some may charge a minimal fee of one to five dollars per night. Most shelters will provide breakfast and dinner. Usually a "soup line" is available close to the shelter for a noon meal. If you are approached for food or shelter in most U.S. cities, you can be sure that for whatever reason that person has not taken advantage of the resources provided for them.

Several years ago in Louisville, Kentucky, a man came by the halfway house that Brenda and I directed and said he was hungry. I had just returned from eating in the soup line with some of the guys in our halfway house. I asked him why I had not seen him at the soup line. He said, "I don't eat in soup lines." My response was that I didn't feed people who didn't eat in soup lines. Needless to say, he left angry.

The Gap in Current Treatments

We always need to be compassionate, and my heart does go out to someone whose pride is keeping him hungry, but we need to learn how to really help people, instead of just making ourselves feel better. There are plenty of resources available, and it is not necessary for us to duplicate resources when all we need to do is find them.

This is also an example of why it is so important to believe what people do, not just what they say. Several times in this book, you will hear this principle. I believe that often the most unloving thing we can do is to believe whatever someone says. The world is filled with people who are professional manipulators, and many of them are drug-addicted.

We need to believe only what the addict does for at least three reasons:

1. In believing only what they do, we take away their power over us. It is virtually impossible to manipulate someone who believes only what you do.
2. We take away a major cause of their own destruction, their ability to manipulate.
3. In order to help those people who legitimately need our help, we need to avoid pouring our efforts into people who cannot yet be helped.

I remember meeting a young man named Philip one day, and as we talked, he really seemed to want to change. He really sounded sincere. He was on drugs and lived in one of the large housing developments in the city. I asked him to attend an AA meeting and bring me back a piece of literature from that meeting signed and dated by the AA chairperson. I told him to meet me the next day at my house at 3:00 P.M. He got there early and waited on the porch. Over the next two weeks he did everything I asked him to do. He came to the CR group, to church, attended some AA meetings and was on time every time. Drug addicts are always on time to purchase their drugs. Being on time for recovery-related activities is an indication that they are willing to invest as much in getting well as they did in their addiction. Within a couple of months, Philip was baptized. He proved he had changed through what he did, not simply what he said.

Brenda and I have often taken strangers into our home and placed ourselves and our children in danger. We have gotten up the next morning with our clothes stolen and the house ransacked. You can chalk that up to being Christlike, or you can figure out that there is a way to be like Jesus and help people while still maintaining your safety and serenity. Today, when we find people in need, we offer to take them to a detox center, a halfway house, a shelter or a soup line. A typical scenario might go like this: I'll take them to the shelter if they will agree to attend an AA meeting the next day, get a newspaper and circle the jobs they think they might be able to do, or go to the Unemployment Office. Then meet me at church, or Bible Talk at a precise time. I ask them to bring the paper or information from their case worker and AA meeting with them. If they do everything I've asked them to do, I continue to invest. If they don't, I tell them that I'll continue to invest when they've done what I asked them to do. They tell me by what they do whether or not I can help them.

Let's turn now to the New York church's CR ministry. I'm discussing this last since our focus is on spiritual recovery. CR is not intended to take the place of more formal types of treatment for those who need it.

Spiritual Treatment—The CR Ministry

The chemical recovery program is typified by "tough love." Each week, the CR group meets in someone's apartment for exactly an hour and a half. Each recovering person is expected to be early and have his discipling partner with him or her. If he or his discipling partner is late, then they are not allowed to stay for the meeting. We don't allow people to explain why they are late because everyone knows that it's only what they do that counts. They are late, period. This prevents excuse-making and manipulation. It is very difficult at times to not let someone in, especially if you know that traffic was particularly bad, or church service ran late. Some may feel that this is not very merciful, but we have learned from experience that being on time with no excuses is a clear indication of a person's motivation to recover.

A brother who graduated from our chemical recovery group shared a story with us that I believe will illustrate this point very well. Before he was a Christian, he was driving into New York City late one night to buy some drugs. He had a brand new car and just as he was crossing the George Washington Bridge, it caught on fire. He abandoned his car burning on the side of the road because he had to be on time to score his drugs. We expect people in our CR groups to demonstrate at least the same degree of eagerness to recover.

Since we only meet once a week, it is imperative that each member's discipling partner attend and that they be on time as well. Sometimes we hear excuses about discipling partners being too busy. While I certainly understand what it's like to be busy, our CR meetings last an hour and a half, once a week. This is life or death, heaven or hell for many who attend. I believe the gravity of the situation demands that someone attend regularly who will devote the time and energy necessary to assist this person in his recovery.

There have been times in the past when leaders have canceled CR because it was Mother's Day or some other special event. I understand that we do this because we view CR as just another meeting, yet for the addict, recovery must come first. For years, they have put everything else first and the results have been disastrous. I tell guys in our groups that if they want to be able to have future Mother's Days, they had better not miss CR. This is not meant as any sort of threat but is meant to sober the person to simply see the reality of the situation.

A few years ago we were in a CR group and a young mother was having a hard time deciding to enter an inpatient treatment program during the holidays. She obviously didn't want to be away from her children on Christmas. I think any of us would probably have been sympathetic to her feelings, but sympathy is not what she needed. One of the women in the group asked her to tell us about last Christmas. Had she been sober? What about the Christmas before that and the one before that. She began to cry. You see how out of touch with reality we can be? What she needed to see was that the best gift she could ever give her family was her own recovery.

The CR meeting consists of the following format: a short devotional, followed by a time of good-news sharing, then usually one or two people read their journals.[4] Group members are expected to give honest feedback with a spirit of genuine concern. Our goals are (1) to help that person assess whether they are really powerless over alcohol or other drugs and (2) to help him to connect pain with using alcohol or drugs. This leads a person to hit bottom, surrender to his powerlessness over drugs and accept his need for God. The goal is to graduate people who are comfortable with being abstinent from alcohol or other drugs.

People who attend the group are expected to begin preparing their journals right away. In addition to writing a journal and listening to others share theirs, three lectures are presented on drugs and spirituality. A person's usual length of stay in a CR group is three to four months, although some may need to stay longer.

CR most resembles an outpatient treatment format, but with two significant differences. First, the recovering disciple brings one of his best friends (discipling partner) with him. Second, he attends several other spiritual meetings a week with the church, which will directly or indirectly help his spiritual recovery.

People who attend CR but relapse may be referred to an additional AA meeting, a detox unit, additional outpatient or even inpatient treatment, depending on the severity and/ or frequency of the relapse(s).

An extremely high percentage of people who complete our CR program as part of their spiritual recovery in the church go on to stay sober, faithful and become extremely productive members of the body of Christ.

8

J O A N N E   R A N D A L L

Codependency Recovery

The Resurrected Life—Part 1

For every person recovering from addiction and for every person still using, there are family and friends around them caught in a related addiction called codependency. Every addict, in order to continue using, needs a helper, an enabler, a rescuer, someone to care for them and insulate them from the pain and consequences of addiction.

Consider the husband who tries to control the reactions and responses of his alcoholic wife. He lies to those around him, saying things are great at home because of his shame. Shame is the base of his every response. He has trouble saying no to people and therefore takes on more than he can reasonably do. Chronically worried about his wife's drinking, he loses his ability to stay focused at work and is often ill with undiagnosed disorders. In retaliation for the lack of control he feels over the addiction, he verbally lashes out at his coworkers and children. His life is out of control. He is physically exhausted, emotionally depressed and spiritually dead.

Consider the wife who drags her husband home from parties, puts him to bed and wakes him up for work in the morning. She works two jobs to keep his irresponsible spending hidden, drives with him when he's drunk, is yelled at and berated for not keeping the house clean, or not keeping the dinner warm when he's an hour late. She has her life threatened in his violent outbursts and is occasionally beaten. She stays with him and is shocked when others encourage her to move out or file a restraining order. Her life, racked by the pain of denial, is out of control. She also is emotionally and spiritually dead.

Around the alcoholic the family functions like a man walking on an injured leg. The injured leg gets supported while the "good leg" takes on the extra load, causing a painful imbalance. What begins as support ends in damage to both legs, destruction of both the addict and the enablers. The devastation of addiction becomes a pattern of thinking and behavior that pervades the entire family unit. The marital relationship becomes a platform to play out the addictive nature of both the alcoholic and the codependent. The alcoholic is addicted to *the alcohol* and the codependent is addicted to *the alcoholic*.

Since marriage among adult codependents is an all-to-common scenario and can be devastating, we will focus our discussion of codependency and recovery on the marital relationship. You will find, however, that many of the recovery steps discussed here will be helpful to other family members caught in the addictive cycle.

Assessment of Codependency

Answer "yes" or "no" to the following critical questions:

1. Do you try to get your spouse to stop drinking by emptying bottles, hiding them, or marking them to see how much he's been drinking?
2. Do you cover up for him when people call and he is passed out, saying he's sick, asleep or not home?
3. Do you scurry around to do all he has asked of

you, to the point of neglecting your own appearance and health?

4. Are you in a continuous state of panic over what he'll be like tonight when he comes home, or even if he'll come home?

5. Do you lose your temper after your spouse has been drinking, then scream at or hit your children over small offenses?

6. Are you deliriously happy and in love with your spouse when you have both planned a special evening together, and then when he doesn't show up, become hateful, bitter and chronically depressed?

7. Do you believe that "it" (some painful episode) will never happen again?

8. Do you feel numb from all you've been through?

9. Do you feel confused, like you are losing your mind?

If you have answered "yes" to even two or three of these questions, you need to consider the possibility that codependency is a problem for you. If there are more than a few "yes" answers, you should seek help now.

Definition

A codependent from a biblical standpoint is a person who prevents others from feeling the consequences of their decisions through control, manipulation, enabling and rescuing. The world perceives a codependent as a person caught up in a behavioral addiction. I believe God sees codependency as a specific group of sins linked together which prevent people from going to heaven. It is far more serious than a behavioral addiction. At the very core, codependency is a lack of trust in God and reveals a heart that has not surrendered. It is sin and it is deadly.

Think about this for a moment: Allowing a person to feel the consequences of the decisions they make can be the best way to drive them toward God. God allows us to bear the consequences of sin as an early-warning system. Consequences are supposed to help us get to heaven by turning us back to God when we are in pain.

Consider the child who decides to show off by standing on his bicycle seat who loses his balance and falls. He runs home to Mom for comfort from the pain. The child has learned a very important lesson in suffering the consequences of foolish behavior. Mom helps her son by reminding him about safety. The memory of the actual pain reminds him and gives him reason to heed the advice. In the same way, God expects us to run to him for comfort and help.

So what does the codependent do? A codependent separates people from the consequences of their sin, much like a mom running alongside of her son's bike, holding it upright as the son dangerously does his stunts. As a result, there is little or no pain associated with this dangerous act. Do you see the connection? The addict feels no pain and thus sees no reason to seek God or to discontinue using drugs or alcohol. The codependent has, in fact, stood in the way of God's plan—the exact opposite of what any disciple should do!

The good news is there is hope. We can change our damaging behavior. We do have control over our own choices. We can decide to trust God's sovereignty, God's foreknowledge and God's way of dealing with the addict. We just need to get out of his way. We need to allow God to be God. Jeremiah 29:11-14 states:

> "For I know the plans I have for you," declares the LORD, "plans to prosper you and not to harm you, plans to give you hope and a future. Then you will

call upon me and come and pray to me, and I will listen to you. You will seek me and find me when you seek me with all your heart. I will be found by you," declares the Lord, "and will bring you back from captivity. I will gather you from all the nations and places where I have banished you," declares the Lord, "and will bring you back to the place from which I carried you into exile."

I am living proof God still carries us out of exile. I am no longer chained to the sin that held me captive. Codependency recovery is a hard road. It takes time and patience. It requires a devotion to God's word and to daily prayer. It takes a commitment not to allow yourself to focus on your spouse's faults, but on your own instead. And it requires a commitment to God not to allow yourself times of unbelief, because God has promised to do more than we could ask or imagine!

Do You Want to Get Well?

Some time later, Jesus went up to Jerusalem for a feast of the Jews. Now there is in Jerusalem near the Sheep Gate a pool, which in Aramaic is called Bethesda and which is surrounded by five covered colonnades. Here a great number of disabled people used to lie—the blind, the lame, the paralyzed. One who was there had been an invalid for thirty-eight years. When Jesus saw him lying there and learned that he had been in this condition for a long time, he asked him, "Do you want to get well?"

"Sir," the invalid replied, "I have no one to help me into the pool when the water is stirred. While I am trying to get in, someone else goes down ahead of me."

> Then Jesus said to him, "Get up! Pick up your
> mat and walk." At once the man was cured; he
> picked up his mat and walked (John 5:1-9a).

I can really relate to the man beside the pool. When I came to really know Jesus I was thirty-two years old. For years I had been blind to the truth. I limped along spiritually. My relationships were all painful, and I was paralyzed by fear. I even had the same type of excuses that he had: It was all someone else's fault! Can you relate? Jesus is asking you the same question he asked the paralytic, the same question he asked me: "Do you want to get well?" He understands your pain but he doesn't want to hear your lack of faith. He knows you've tried, but you've never tried his way with his power! His way requires you to admit you are powerless and he is all powerful. His way requires you to take responsibility for your own recovery: to pick up your mat (not someone else's) and walk. Are you ready? Are you sick and tired of being "sick and tired"? Then let's follow Jesus' path to recovery!

Powerlessness

In Luke 14:33 Jesus challenges us to give up everything in order to follow him. One of the hardest things for people to actually give up and give over to God is control of their lives. This requires knowing God well enough to trust him in everything. When we say "God is in control; he is all powerful," what we are admitting is that we are not. We are, in fact, out of control. We are saying God has the power, therefore I am powerless. As with chemical recovery, the first step in codependency recovery is developing a deep sense of our own powerlessness to accomplish anything without God.

The Powerlessness of Codependency

It is important to see the futility in our thinking that we can control others' lives. Listen to the powerlessness in the following accounts.

I can't stop thinking about what he might do the next time he's drunk. I must not make him angry. The house has to be spotless, the dinner perfect, and I can't be late. There's so much to worry about. I don't see how I can let go and let God handle it!

> We know that the law is spiritual; but I am unspiritual, sold as a slave to sin (Romans 7:14).

Last week my husband came home and beat me in front of the kids. Yesterday, he passed out in the bathroom with a needle in his arm. My son found him lying on the floor in his own vomit. I was advised to file for a restraining order to protect me and the kids but when I went to do it, I suddenly felt like I was being so cruel. Going behind his back will only make him angrier. I know I should leave, but who will take care of him?

> I do not understand what I do. For what I want to do I do not do, but what I hate I do (Romans 7:15).

My wife has been drinking rather heavily for a few months now. I've talked to her about not drinking so much, but she gives me this sweet look and convinces me it won't happen again, that I'm making a big deal over nothing. I feel like I should get some advice about this, but I don't want to upset or embarrass her. Each time I decide to mention it, I chicken out.

> I know that nothing good lives in me, that is, in my sinful nature. For I have the desire to do what is good, but I cannot carry it out (Romans 7:18).

One of the key factors in identifying our own powerlessness is in identifying the underlying sin. If we were really in control, we could rationally see these sins in our lives and just decide not to commit them. When we are powerless, it's not that simple.

The Sins of Codependency

> ...it is no longer I myself who does it, but it is sin living in me (Romans 7:17).

The following sins are often associated with those who enable the addict. These sins are often linked together and appear in cycles.

Envy—Do you envy those with Christian spouses?

Bitterness—Are you nursing and rehearsing all the times you were hurt?

Rage—When was the last time you lost control of your anger?

Arrogance—Do you believe the addict is to blame for all your pain?

Cowardice—Do you fear taking steps towards recovery?

Idolatry—Are you consumed with thoughts of the addict?

Resentment—Do you resent the fact that you are at fault also?

Malice—Do you plan traps for the addict to prove you are right about his abuse?

Lying—Do you lie to cover up the shame?

Faithlessness—Do you really believe God wants to help you and your spouse?

From Powerlessness to Empowerment

Within the list of sin and examples above, you can hear the powerlessness: You desire what is good but you are powerless to stop yourself from the fatal pattern of giving in to sin. Yet, there is hope. As in everything, Jesus has the answers.

In Gethsemane we watch Jesus struggle, fight off the temptation to flee and surrender to God's will. By imitating

Jesus we too can overcome our codependent nature. We too, can resist the sins of codependency. Look carefully at the steps he took in Matthew 26:36-46.

1. He is open and honest with his friends about how he feels (v. 38):
   - Jesus is overwhelmed.
   - Jesus is depressed to the point of wanting to die.
2. He humbles himself in every way (emotionally, physically and spiritually) before God (v. 39a).
3. He calls on God to change the situation, if he is willing (v. 39b).
4. He calls on God for strength to endure and not back down from the challenges God has set before him (v. 42).
5. He prays again the same thing (v. 44).
6. Jesus rises resolute (completely committed to his course of action) to do God's will no matter what (v. 46).

Jesus' Actions	Actions Of Recovery
Open and Humble	Admit Powerlessness
↓	↓
Pray Pray Pray	Surrender
↓	↓
Rise to Do God's Will	Empowered by Holy Spirit

Paul cries out in Romans: "What a wretched man I am! Who will rescue me from this body of death? Thanks be to God—through Jesus Christ our Lord!" (7:24-25a). So who is our Savior? It's Jesus. Who has come to help us overcome our deepest, darkest moments of despair? Jesus. Who died to wash all this wretched sin away? It's Jesus. He's our living hope. He has shown us the way. It is our responsibility to follow him.

Hopefully you see now that the problem in your life is not just your spouse's drinking or drug use, but it is the sin living in you. Admission of sin on our part is always the first step we need to take as disciples. Look carefully and you will find that the sin in your life is as out of control as that of the addict. You are both on a runaway train and without the help of God, this train is going to crash!

In a diary I had kept before I became a disciple, I wrote this passage one night in my own personal Gethsemane:

> I never realized Satan could be so strong and could so seductively lure me away from what I know is right. I feel as though part of me has died and in doing so, has destroyed my self-esteem and self-respect. I'm terrified by my inability to walk away from it all. I pray, O God, you will not abandon me here. I need all your strength to lift me up out of this great black abyss into which I have fallen. Carry me until I am able to stand. Hold my hand until I am able to balance. Never leave me without your vision of who you are and who I am to you and what I am here on earth to do. God, cleanse me and make me whole again.

Do you hear the powerlessness? I was on the floor crying when I wrote this. I was open about my desperation. I was humbled by the depth of my sin. I was praying and asking God to show me his way. I was Romans 7:14! And even though I didn't realize it, I was imitating Jesus in Gethsemane. Three months later I met disciples who would help me to become a Christian. God heard my prayer, reached out and made me whole again.

The great news is that Jesus wants to overcome the powerlessness for you, too. Isaiah 42:16 says:

> I will lead the blind by ways they have not known,
>   along unfamiliar paths I will guide them;
> I will turn the darkness into light before them
>   and make the rough places smooth.
> These are the things I will do;
>   I will not forsake them (Isaiah 42:16).

'I Tell You the Truth'

By far the most important step in overcoming denial is in separating God's truth from the lies we tell ourselves and the lies others bombard us with. We have just learned the truth about our powerlessness and enslavement to sin. Do you see the truth about your spouse's alcoholism or drug addiction? This was very hard for me to accept. Growing up in today's drinking culture will blind you to what normal drinking behavior is, but seeing the truth destroys our denial and thus destroys Satan's stronghold over our emotional addiction. Consider the normal and alcoholic behaviors shown in figure 3.

Most of us spend years in denial because the truth brings pain with it. We don't want to deal with the fact that someone we love is an alcoholic or drug addict. We don't want to see that we should take action to protect ourselves and our children from the violence that ensues. We don't want to admit our lives are so out of control. Instead we fashion a life in our minds that does not exist. Are we not as much to blame for the critical path we are on as the one using? We look for freedom in a lie. As Romans 1:25 says,

> They exchanged the truth of God for a lie, and worshipped and served created things rather than the Creator—who is forever praised.

Normal	Alcoholic
• Has an occasional drink with a meal.	• Drinks to feel the effect, to relax, to avoid life.
• Rarely, if ever, gets drunk.	• Nearly always gets drunk or buzzed.
• No negative consequences.	• Consequences include: vomiting, hangovers, drunk-driving arrests, relationship break downs, violent behavior, job loss, injuries and blackouts.
• Holds a job.	• 95% of all alcoholics/drug addicts hold a job.
• Can quit anytime.	• Quit many times, but always goes back even after prolonged periods of abstinence.
• Drinking pattern remains the same.	• Drinking pattern is progressive. This increased intake results in more consequences. Consequences develop slowly but steadily and result in mental, physical, emotional and spiritual devastation.

Figure 3

Not only are we lying, we are actually worshiping and serving the alcoholic in desperate attempts to receive attention and love in return. This is idolatry, and it is fruitless.

Jesus says freedom can only be found in the truth (John 8:31-32). Studying these passages opened my eyes and cut my heart. I desperately wanted to be free—free from the lies, free from hiding who I really was, free from the anxieties that strangled me. Mike Leatherwood challenged me with it all when he said, "Joanne, you are a liar, and your whole life is a lie." I was enslaved to the dreamy life I had made up in my head. My real life was filled with pain and deception. I lied about everything, even things that didn't matter. I would either minimize my sin or exaggerate how I was victimized by someone else's sin. I left things out or I kept silent, but the result was always the same: a deception. Nothing I ever said was the absolute truth. Yet I am not unique. This is the classic example of the addictive thinking and behavior seen among addicts and codependents alike.

Learning to Tell the Truth

In order to tell the truth, ask yourself the following questions:

1. How are you feeling about your spouse's addiction? (Pick a feeling: mad, sad, glad, afraid, embarrassed.)
2. Do you say to yourself, "I'm not supposed to feel this way, so I don't"?
3. How often do you say: "I'm doing fine." "No, I don't need any help." Are these the truth or lies?
4. What have you said today that is deceptive? Go back and tell the whole truth.
5. Do you feel more comfortable with the lie than you do with the truth?

Challenge yourself today to tell the truth about how you really feel, what is really going on inside your head, your heart and behind your front door. Learn to hate the lies by seeing how we first deceive ourselves and then others. Deception offends God and aids others in their denial. It is the truth that will set you free. The great thing about sharing your feelings is that you realize that we all have them. Some are positive. Some are negative. But whatever they turn out to be, it is important that we acknowledge them first, then we can work on turning the negative, unhealthy feelings around with God's word. The freedom that comes with telling the truth is you can now say, "I want you to know me."

Emotional Blackouts

Jesus did an intensely powerful thing when he told the truth: He overcame the power of Satan. Satan has an incredible hold on our lives when we live with an alcoholic or drug addict. He stands in our face yelling his lies:

"You never do anything right," or "You're so stupid," or "You're a terrible excuse for a wife." When Satan attacks this way, the codependent goes into what I call an "emotional blackout." We no longer see clearly. The truth is lost in a cascade of negative feelings. We believe the lies we hear from Satan, and in our minds God becomes small and powerless. We believe that God is not able to rescue us. We become paralyzed.

In Numbers 14:1-4 we see the Israelites go into an emotional blackout.

> That night all the people of the community raised their voices and wept aloud. All the Israelites grumbled against Moses and Aaron, and the whole assembly said to them, "If only we had died in Egypt! Or in this desert! Why is the LORD bringing us to this land only to let us fall by the sword? Our wives and children will be taken as plunder. Wouldn't it be better for us to go back to Egypt?" And they said to each other, "We should choose a leader and go back to Egypt" (Numbers 14:1-4).

The Life Application Bible points out that the people's greatest fears were being realized. They lost their perspective and forgot who God really was. You see, their "god" was small. They forgot that the real God is strong. He is always strong, always faithful, always powerful and always the same. They forgot that God was in control of their situation. They believed only by sight, not by faith. They emotionally "blacked out." Their foolish hearts were darkened (Romans 1:21), and they couldn't see the truth through the blackening cloud of emotion. They had lost their faith and were now blind to the truth.

The people had grumbled, wept aloud, raised their voices, and pulled the entire crowd into their emotional nightmare. Look at the amount of negative energy they were willing to expend grumbling and complaining, to the point of choosing new leaders to go back to Egypt! The truth was that they did not want to endure any more pain. They wanted to quit. How often do you "go back to Egypt" in your emotional blackouts rather than being faithful and utilizing this energy to move forward? Are you more like the Israelites than you would like to admit?

It may be helpful to follow these steps in order not to "black out" emotionally and spiritually:

1. Write out your feelings about the situation.
2. Take those emotions captive. *Stop.* Do not act on them, just put them on hold for a moment.
3. Destroy the lies with God's word and promises. Look for the real truth hidden within the lie. "You always" and "You never" are almost always followed by a lie. "Usually" is more the real case. Remember, just because you do not do something right doesn't make you a terrible wife, a terrible husband, or a terrible parent.
4. Study out a person in the Bible who overcame a similar situation (such as intense persecution) or has a similar character to yours. Examine his or her faith, prayer, and conviction.
5. Read and reread Isaiah 41:9-13, with your name placed in, until you believe deep in your heart that God has placed great value on *you*!

The Word is so powerful! I know of nothing else that can steer my perspective away from the lies to the truth. Use it always as your compass out of the darkness and into the light whenever you find yourself in the tempest of an emotional blackout.

9

J O A N N E   R A N D A L L

Codependency Recovery

The Resurrected Life—Part 2

As with drugs and alcohol, the key to recovery from codependency is clearly seeing your powerlessness and telling the whole truth. A codependency journal will aid you in revealing the truth about your patterns of sin and your level of denial. It will get you in touch with what is really happening in your relationship with the addict and the feelings that have been suppressed for so long.

The Codependency Journal

The Format

Write down every single drinking or drug episode you have witnessed or been affected by, from the very first incident until the present. In each event describe the following: (1) what the person drank/used and how much; (2) what happened; (3) what you did; and (4) how you felt about what you did. (Feelings generally fall into one of these five categories: mad, sad, glad, afraid, embarrassed.)

Writing the journal is one of the most difficult steps in the recovery process. It forces us out of the darkness and into the light. It exposes all we have worked so hard to suppress. It brings us to the realization that we haven't really been open with our feelings about anything in a very long time.

Dealing with Fear

Many people may procrastinate or freeze in fear at this point in the journal writing, but encouragement can be taken from the scriptures. Consider 1 John 4:18:

> There is no fear in love. But perfect love drives out fear, because fear has to do with punishment. The one who fears is not made perfect in love.

God, who is perfect love, drives out our fears. Let go of fear and hold on to faith in Jesus and the feelings and events will flood back to your memory. Cling to Jesus, and he will enable you to move forward and grow.

Reading the Journal

The journal may be read to a codependency group that is following the steps described in this book, or it can be read to strong, mature Christian leaders (at least two) who can provide godly feedback in the areas described below. Preface the journal reading by letting the group know it is very difficult to open up like this. Help the group be sensitive. Do not allow anyone to take notes. Anyone who wants to give feedback should do so in the first person. For example,

> "I can really relate to how angry you felt when your husband came home that drunk and violent. But what I have learned is that my angry responses only fuel the fire of my husband's anger. Jesus never allowed his actions to be reactions. Planning my responses before he walks in the door helps me."

The group should listen for the following :

- Progression of alcoholism/addiction in spouse
- Patterned responses to certain types of situations
- Blame-shifting

- Manipulation and control on the part of the codependent
- Whether the person is in touch with his or her feelings
- Victim mentality
- Rescuing addict from consequences
- Surrender—accepts that he or she is powerless to change the addict
- Acceptance of truth about his or her marriage
- Taking responsibility for his or her part in the destruction of the relationship
- Willingness to rely on Jesus for help

The main goal is to have the reader connect the pain he feels with his attempts to control and manipulate the alcoholic. The reader needs to see his own sin associated with rescuing the alcoholic from the consequences, thereby preventing him from hitting bottom and seeking help.

What you look for is a person cut by the sins associated with his codependency, a person eager to repent because of how he has hurt God and hurt the addict by softening the consequences, to the point where the addict does not pursue recovery or pursue God. You look for the heart of the lost son as he returns to his father (Luke 15:17-21).

If the writer has not gotten in touch with his feelings or does not connect with the pain or did not follow the specified format, you must ask him to rewrite the journal and reread it the following week. This is critical because a person cannot recover on his own terms. He must be surrendered to the recovery process. As he writes and reads his journal, he will begin to see that his terms did not work. Use the journal to open his eyes to the fallacy of his thinking patterns and use the Scriptures to correct these patterns.

Dealing with Shame

Very often after reading their journals, people are struck by some very strong feelings. The feelings that they spent a lifetime protecting are now out! The mask is gone, and they begin to feel very vulnerable. They now see the lies they designed and rehearsed day after day. They see the devastation in their marriage and other relationships. What should be felt as guilt is overcome by shame. People often confuse guilt and shame, so let's take a moment to define each.

Guilt is a feeling we get when we make a mistake, go beyond the boundaries, break the law or sin. The godly response to guilt is to take the necessary corrective action to get back in line (i.e., repent). Shame is a feeling of total disgrace, feeling self-condemned or condemned by others. All these feelings can be debilitating. The typical response to shame is to feel as though *you* are a mistake, rather than feeling that you have made a mistake. Guilt is not necessarily a negative feeling. Its purpose is to help us feel the boundaries of right and wrong. Guilt acts as an alarm to signal us back onto the path of righteousness. Shame, on the other hand, is the condemnation of your whole being. Psalm 25:1-3 explains that shame is reserved for those who refuse to follow God. Those who love God and follow him will never be put to shame:

> To you, O LORD, I lift up my soul;
>   in you I trust, O my God.
> Do not let me be put to shame,
>   nor let my enemies triumph over me.
> No one whose hope is in you
>   will ever be put to shame,
> but they will be put to shame
>   who are treacherous without excuse
>   (Psalm 25:1-3).

One of the most effective strategies I have found in destroying Satan's power over my feelings of shame is to write down exactly how I feel. We need to be honest with ourselves and with God. Once written, we can attack the lies line-by-line with God's word and replace them with the truth. Shame comes from not having a healthy understanding of who you are to God and who God has created you to be. Studying the scriptures and the scriptural principles below can renew your mind and deeply encourage you.[1]

> I am a new creation (2 Corinthians 5:17).
> I am a child of God, and I belong to him (John 1:12; 1 Peter 2:9).
> I am a gift from God to Jesus (John 17:9,12, 24).
> I am greatly loved (Romans 8:35-39).
> I have been drawn to God by his will (John 6:44).
> God works for my good and he has called me according to his purpose (Romans 8:28).
> I am predestined to be conformed to the likeness of his son (Romans 8:29).
> By renewing my mind with the Word I can test and approve what God's will is (Romans 12:2).
> I have been chosen before the creation to be holy and blameless (Ephesians 1:4).
> I am in Jesus' prayers (John 17:9; Hebrews 7:25).
> I have been washed, sanctified and justified in the name of Jesus (1 Corinthians 6:11).
> I am co-heir with Christ (Romans 8:17).
> I have been set free from sin and am a slave to righteousness (Romans 6:18).
> His divine power has given me everything I need for life and godliness (2 Peter 1:3).
> For God so loved the world that he gave his one and only son, so that when I believed in him I would not perish but have eternal life (John 3:16).

Surrender

Completing the journal and reading it aloud helps you surrender. Surrender occurs when we realize the only control we have is found in the decision to move toward God (surrender) or away from him (rebellion). It occurs when we are willing to trust God's way and not our own (Proverbs 3:5-6). It occurs when we realize that our role is not in controlling others, and we are at peace with this. Surrender occurs when we have been humbled by God and are deeply grateful to be given everlasting life. It is only from the vantage point of surrender that we begin to see the awesome grace and power of God in all situations. Amazing grace becomes just that—amazing.

One of the most stunning examples of surrender I've ever seen was during Operation Desert Storm, when Iraqi soldiers surrendered to the Americans. The Iraqi soldiers were on their knees, hands tied behind their backs, kissing the boots of the American soldiers. They were begging for their lives to be spared. It was then that I realized this is what we are to be like before the cross of Jesus—totally humbled, without the right to bargain, desperately needing grace.

Surrender is a willingness to face the painful truth of who we are and what we have become without God and put absolute trust in Jesus to control our lives. God is clearly trustworthy (Psalm 139:16), but we hold out for so long. We are like performers hanging from a trapeze over a pool of pain. We believe we are solidly in control of our lives, but the truth is we hang there out of fear, terrified to let go for fear we will die in the pain. Yet the only way to really be set free is to let go of the trapeze, trust in Jesus and swim through the pool of pain. Proverbs 3:5-6 tells us:

> Trust in the Lord with all your heart
> and lean not on your own understanding.

> In all your ways acknowledge him,
>   and he will make your paths straight.

Since we are human, our thinking is, by definition, fallible. God's word is based on absolute truth and a God who is absolutely trustworthy. Clearly we need to let go of our thinking and take hold of God's wisdom.

Surrender requires us to be led by Jesus. Psalm 23 says, "He leads me beside quiet waters" (v. 2). "He guides me in paths of righteousness" (v. 3). Do you see how the initiative is with the shepherd Jesus, not us, to lead? If you have surrendered you can be led by him. God has promised us he will lead us in the best ways. Philippians 1:6 says: "being confident of this, that he who began a good work in you will carry it on to completion."

Are You Surrendered?

Ask yourself these questions to see if you are really surrendered. When adversity strikes:

1. Do you find yourself unable to love the person who is the instrument of that adversity?
2. Are you able to forgive them?
3. Are you trusting God's plan to guide you during these times?
4. Can you see the unbelief and resentment surge within you when adversity strikes?
5. Do you put the demands of your spouse above God's commands?

Don't shrink back from the awesome lesson of discipline because Hebrews 12:11 says, "a harvest of righteousness and peace [is promised] for those who have been trained by it." You cannot be transformed into the likeness of Christ without the evil in your heart being exposed. And in cases such as the journal, God is going deeper than making us conscious of a specific sin. He wants to get at the root cause: our sinful nature manifested in the rebellion of our will against his. The world has taught us self-reliance and independence; these are the lies of Satan. God reveals how our real idol is ourselves and how spiritually ignorant and helpless we really are without him. Begin to set things straight and make God your only Lord, not your spouse or yourself.

When Jesus is truly our Lord, there can be no terms in surrender, no compromise, no deals made, no limits placed. God gives us a clear plan: (1) humbly pray for forgiveness for assuming control; (2) confess idolatry, and ask to be held accountable; and (3) repent minute-by-minute, hour-by-hour and day-by-day to stay surrendered.

If lack of surrender is a real issue for you, I suggest reading the book *Trusting God* by Jerry Bridges,[2] which gives an awesome description of the nature and character of God and why he can be trusted, even in difficult circumstances. Also read *The Victory of Surrender* by Gordon Ferguson,[3] who goes through a step-by-step process in developing a truly surrendered heart.

Rescuing/Enabling

Read the Parable of the Lost Son in Luke 15:11-24. Look at the kind of love the father had for his son. It was a "letting go" kind of love. Don't you think the father knew his son would squander his money out in the world? I'm sure he did. But he gave him what was his and let him go. Do you think it was painful to let him go? You bet it was. But he was willing to endure the pain, knowing the consequences could change his son's life! He didn't control his son or manipulate him, and he didn't go with his son and share in his defeat. Does he search for him when the famine gets intense? No! What he does is watch and wait for his son to return home humbled, broken and changed.

Look what it took for the son to come to his senses (v. 17). He was near starvation and had already lost everything. He only noticed he was in need during the famine but he continued to scheme. He may have thought, "Oh, let's see, I'll hire myself out to feed pigs" (from v. 15). (To the law-keeping Jews to whom Jesus told this parable, there wasn't anything much lower than serving pigs.) It was utter starvation that drove him to his knees, and only then did he recognize how desperately he needed his father. The key to him coming to his senses was that "no one gave him anything" (v. 16). No one rescued him. No one enabled him to keep going on this foolish path. He was a man feeling the consequences of his decisions. It was those very circumstances, as they worsened, that ultimately drove him back home, a humble, broken and surrendered man.

What consequences were severe enough for the lost son to come to his senses? How does this translate into what it will take for your spouse? There are costs to count in order to let go. Are you willing to trust God enough to allow the painful consequences to happen?

The Endless Cycles

These are the two powerlessness cycles of the codependent and the alcoholic. The codependent functions within the Rescue/Enabling Cycle while the alcoholic functions within the Addiction Cycle. Both cycles feed off one another spiraling downward. Here is what the Rescue/Enabling and Addiction cycles look like:

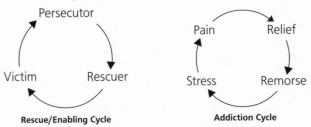

Figure 4. Rescue/Enabling and Addiction Cycles

The addict feels like his life is burdened (*pain*), and he deserves a drink (*relief*). He comes home at 3:00 A.M. and can't get up the next day for work (*remorse*). You enable him by rousing him, giving him coffee to sober him up and get him ready for work. You call his boss and make excuses about why he'll be late. You tell the kids, "Daddy's not feeling well so he can't go to the Boy Scout meeting with you tonight" (*rescuer*).

You have just rescued him from all the negative consequences of using. Then, annoyed at all your fussing and control, he yells at you anyway and decides not to go to work at all (*stress*). Because he won't conform to your plan of how things should be played out, you feel victimized (*victim*) and you retaliate by persecuting him for his alcohol abuse (*persecutor*). He then feels justified to use again because of the pain he feels and goes out and gets drunk (*pain*). Initially, he feels better. He gets relief from the pain by continuing to medicate his feelings through using. But when he sobers up, he feels remorseful about how he's hurting his family or himself and promises that it will never happen again. This is sometimes called the "hearts and flowers" stage. But as the stress of daily life continues, he finds he cannot cope. The pain increases, and he uses again. You continue to rescue and feel victimized. The cycles continue together in a downward spiral of abuse.

Although it seems that the enabler is intervening to help the addict, people actually enable in order to meet their own needs. According to Al J. Mooney, M.D. in *The Recovery Book*:

> [Enabling is] an attempt to restabilize the relationship, to counter growing alienation, to lure the addict back into the relationship by providing a counterforce to the drugs that seem to be tugging

the other way. [Enabling] not only doesn't succeed
in keeping the marriage together, it allows [the ad-
diction] to progress to a more serious stage and
worsen prognosis for recovery.[4]

The only way to recovery is to *stop rescuing!* The user
will find himself without the support necessary to continue
without severe consequences. That gives him a choice, to
clean up the ravages of his life by turning to God, or to die
immobilized beneath it. It's a tough-love theory that saved
both my husband and me from disaster. It will save your
sanity and help your spouse feel the consequences of his or
her alcohol abuse. Listen carefully to what I'm telling you:
Every time your spouse uses, you make up the difference. If
he passes out at night, you make excuses. You lie to your
children, but they know the truth. You say "Everything is
fine," but it's not fine at all. If you are living with a person
who uses illegal drugs and you have no money to eat or pay
rent, how can it be fine? If your spouse is an abusive alcoholic, how can it be fine? "It is fine" is a lie. Furthermore,
what you are really doing is helping him kill himself. This is
absolutely *not* biblical love. Listen to God's advice in Ezekiel
3:18-19:

> When I say to a wicked man, "You will surely die"
> and you do not warn him or speak out to dissuade
> him from his evil ways in order to save his life, that
> wicked man will die for his sin, and I will hold you
> accountable for his blood. But if you do warn the
> wicked man and he does not turn from his wicked-
> ness or from his evil ways, he will die for his sin, but
> you will have saved yourself.

Remember the runaway train? It's going to crash. All
addicts, if they continue to use, die drunk, die from over-
dose, die from diseases associated with alcoholism or com-

mit suicide. You have a choice, warn the addict and get off the train yourself, or die with him.

Taking the Pillow Away

In order to save his life and yours, it is critical that you stop rescuing the addict from the consequences of his actions. Imitate the father in the Parable of the Lost Son. Only pain brings a person out of denial. Take the pillow away, and let him fall. If he loses his job, he will feel the pain. If someone calls, hand him the phone, drunk, sober or asleep. He must face his life. If he uses all the money, open your own personal bank account and put your paycheck in it. Use this for food and half of the rent. If he spends all his and can't pay, you can ask him where it went. Hold him accountable. Tell him the truth about his drug or alcohol abuse. Encourage him to get help as you get help. Tell him you love him, but you can have nothing to do with his drinking or drugging. If you are in an abusive situation, first seek the wisest and most godly counsel you can find. Then Sam and Geri Laing in their book, *Friends and Lovers* suggest that you follow these guidelines:

1. Do not compromise your commitment to God, his church, the law or your conscience.
2. Do your best to deal forthrightly and firmly with your husband yourself.
3. If you are in a position of physical danger, get out of it.
4. If you are in a position in which you are being destroyed as a person, either work for change or remove yourself from the situation. (Separation should be a last resort and hopefully only a temporary one.)
5. Retain a respectful attitude toward your husband, even when you must confront him with his wrongdoing.[5]

What I am describing here is biblical love. God allows us to go to the pit. He does not empty bottles or manipulate our behavior, nor does he take the temptation away. God gives us a choice, and he allows us to choose our own path. We must do the same with our spouses.

In the end God will prepare a great celebration feast. He will kill the fattened calf. He will be filled with compassion and joy at your loved one's return. He will call you "good and faithful servant" because you imitated his actions and heart and helped bring his "lost son" home by letting go!

Developing a Plan

If you are convicted about no longer rescuing your spouse from the consequences of his drinking or drug use, you need a plan—a plan for the next time your spouse comes home drunk or high, a plan to keep yourself out of the rescuing cycle, and a plan to keep the truth in front of you so that denial doesn't lull you into believing this is the last time. Having an established plan is like a fire drill. Fire drills are performed so that you don't need to think in the midst of a fire. You just act. The thinking was all done calmly, prior to the fire, therefore you can trust your actions in a crisis and be confident of your decisions.

This plan is, in essence, an informal intervention. You are intervening into the progression of the addiction to raise the pain of the consequences to a point where the addict might "hit bottom" and recover.

Abstinence for the Codependent?

The first step is to decide if you, the codependent, want to abstain from all alcoholic beverages and mood-altering drugs (including cigarettes) yourself. This is by far the best show of support you can make. It is a personal choice, but I believe it is difficult to take a stand against the addict's drug and alcohol abuse when you drink and smoke in front of him. Paul knew this principle when he addressed the church in Corinth.

> Be careful, however, that the exercise of your freedom does not become a stumbling block to the weak. When you sin against your brothers in this way and wound their weak conscience, you sin against Christ. Therefore, if what I eat causes my brother to fall into sin, I will never eat meat again, so that I will not cause him to fall (1 Corinthians 8:9, 12-13).

Reasonable Consequences

Next, you need to put a plan together for what the consequences will be the next time your spouse comes home drunk or high. Plan ahead. As discussed earlier, *get advice!* Decide what you want to do. Will you ask him to leave, or will you leave when he comes home drunk again? Which friends will you stay with? How long will you stay away, and on what conditions will you return? Consider what you would do if you were out with your spouse and he or she used. Would you take a cab home, or arrange ahead of time for someone to be available to pick you up? Count the cost of the consequences for yourself. Are you willing to face the consequences, too? Remember, in order for us to be saved, Jesus had to face the cross. For everyone that follows Jesus there is a price for helping others to be saved!

Put a script together to discuss the consequences with your spouse while he is sober so he knows what they will be and will have an opportunity to comply and seek help for himself. For the most part, the best time to discuss the plan is when he is hung over or sick. Alcoholic spouses are usually feeling the most remorseful about their drinking and have the greatest need to quit at this time. Again, seek godly advice. It is very important at this point because in very violent situations it may be best to get a restraining order from the courts without your spouse's knowledge and let the police speak with him. In other cases, your plan may be to take yourself to a battered women's shelter. There is a toll-free number in every city phone book. This may be best if the husband is extremely violent and may know where to look for you. In other less violent situations, you can discuss the plan outlined below with him.

Putting the Plan into Action

After establishing a plan and preparing ahead (enlisting friends willing to let you stay, putting a cab fund together, including developing a formal intervention plan and seeking wise counsel), you are now ready to take action. As with anything else, before you confront the addict, pray! I memorized these verses in Jeremiah to calm my fears about saying the "wrong thing."

> "Ah, Sovereign LORD," I said, "I do not know how to speak; I am only a child."
>
> But the LORD said to me, "Do not say, 'I am only a child.' You must go to everyone I send you to and say whatever I command you. Do not be afraid of them, for I am with you and will rescue you," declares the LORD.
>
> Then the LORD reached out his hand and touched my mouth and said to me, "Now, I have put my words in your mouth."
>
> "Get yourself ready! Stand up and say to them whatever I command you. Do not be terrified by them, or I will terrify you before them. They will fight against you but will not overcome you, for I am with you and will rescue you," declares the LORD (Jeremiah 1:6-9, 17, 19).

The discussion should include these elements:

- Share how you cannot live like this any longer.
- Share how you are getting help.
- Share your desire to see him get help.
- Discuss the consequences for drinking/drugging such as:
    - if you drink in the house, the children and I will leave,
    - if you come home drunk/high, the children and I will leave,
    - if we go somewhere and you drink, I'll take a cab home.
- Express your love for him or her, your desire to see the family stay together, your desire to see him be all he can be.
- Share your vision of who he could become with God's help.
- Express your desire for him to be comforted by God's forgiveness as you have been.
- Give him a chance to repent, but be prepared to follow through if he doesn't. Remember, repentance is seen in actions, not words alone. Repentance is not about good intentions. It is about real change. True repentance is always proved by our deeds (Acts 26:20).

If you find you are unable to commit yourself to follow through, then you are not as resolute as Jesus was in Gethsemane, nor are you surrendered to God's power to work through the situation. Go back and review the surrender section of this chapter and be assured that God does have the power to do a tremendous miracle here if you have the faith to see it through. Also know that God has already determined the outcome of the plan. Proverbs 21:1 reminds us that "the king's heart is in the hand of the Lord," not in your hand!

I have often seen women take action based on an intellectual agreement with the advice they received. So when they try to follow through and stand on the convictions of others, it *does not work*. Their plan is foiled by their own lack of faith and inability to be committed to the full course of action. It is better by far to wait and work through to true surrender than to plow ahead into a course of action you cannot, in your heart of hearts, follow through with. The negative outcome of such an attempt can destroy your very best opportunity of intervening effectively.

The plan outlined above is the plan that I have used in my life and it has worked for me. Remember each and every situation varies. Pray fervently that God gives you his wisdom to proceed the way he sees best in your particular situation. Listen to Paul's advice in Philippians 1:9-11 when he says:

> And this is my prayer: that your love may abound more and more in knowledge and depth of insight, so that you may be able to discern what is best and may be pure and blameless until the day of Christ, filled with the fruit of righteousness that comes through Jesus Christ—to the glory and praise of God (Philippians 1:9-11).

Remember the great heroes of the Bible, like Joseph and David. They were taken captive, betrayed, forgotten and treated unfairly, but they never compromised their relationship with God, nor did they ever doubt his hand in all that transpired, even when it took years for their situations to improve. Their stories are told to encourage you and to show you how trustworthy our God is. They have taught us that faithfulness and righteousness, despite the circumstances, begins with each of us individually.

Possible Outcomes

Because of the impending consequences, the addict may change his behavior. He may even stop using for a while. But if he does not join a recovery group or seriously study the Bible and put it into practice, this is really only a worldly type of sorrow. You should anticipate anger and resentment on his part, even though he may not be using. AA calls this a "dry drunk" or "white knuckling." This is by no means recovery! You may see the addict switch addictions, using pills, workaholism, cigarettes, overeating or delving into pornography because the true sins of addiction have not been dealt with. You can definitely expect the alcoholic to become increasingly manipulative and work hard to wear down your resolve to follow through with your plan.

Pray daily, fervently and faithfully. Pray with others in the same situation. Cry out together to God. Pray that God breaks him of his addiction. Pray you will be able to love him through it. Pray for strength for your family to endure and be faithful whatever God's plan is. Stand firmly committed to the plan. You are his and your children's only hope of breaking the continuing cycle of addiction. Isaiah 54:13-14 says,

> All your sons will be taught by the LORD,
>   and great will be your children's peace.
> In righteousness you will be established:
> Tyranny will be far from you;
>   you will have nothing to fear.
> Terror will be far removed;
>   it will not come near you.

I discussed a plan similar to the one described here with my husband, and he agreed to it. For nine months he neither came home drunk nor did he drink at home. He also agreed to go to AA but did not follow through. Then, one day, a violent episode occurred. I decided to put my plan into action. I took the children, the suitcase I had packed nine months before (albeit with the wrong season's clothes!) and left. My conviction was that love always protects (1 Corinthians 13:7), and I felt the need to protect myself and my children from any potential violence. We stayed at a friend's house (as per my plan) that night. The next morning when I awoke I thought about what it would be like living alone without my husband, without my house, without the car and how the boys would feel without their father. Then I thought about God, and that one thought brought contentment. I still had my God, and my God had protected me from harm. I was still a disciple, and I would be a disciple no matter where I lived or what my circumstances were. I realized for the first time the joy of having treasure in heaven. No one, no matter how violent, could take my God from me.

My husband and I were separated for the next four weeks. It was a deeply painful time for both of us. We had been married for ten years, and we had dated for eight years before that. Watching our marriage fall apart was very painful. But during the separation he was able to come to terms with his alcoholism. He had a lot to figure out. First he realized he couldn't recover living with us. I also had a lot to figure out. I realized I wasn't helping his recovery, and during the separation I prayed and studied the Scriptures. He went to AA meetings three times a day during that time and traveled to New Jersey to see Mike Leatherwood. Mike encouraged him to study the Bible, and he did. He went through the chemical recovery program. As of this writing he has been sober five years!

Rebuilding Your Foundation on Jesus

God has transformed my relationship with my husband. We began as a couple about to destroy each other and have ended up at peace and best friends. Proverbs 16:7 says "When a man's ways are pleasing to the Lord, he makes even his enemies live at peace with him." I know God has great plans in store for all of us (Jeremiah 29:11). Yet to accomplish these great plans, God has had to teach us tremendous lessons in destroying old idols, overcoming hateful, critical attitudes and building new attitudes of forgiveness and grace.

Destroying Old Idols

Once in recovery, seeing how a godly marital relationship works is a great step in establishing a new standard in your own relationship with your spouse and ultimately finding lasting peace. In this respect, Sam and Geri Laing's book *Friends and Lovers* is a "must read." They explain how God heads the family, led by the husband and supported by the wife. The expectation that our spouse is to meet our every need has to be destroyed. No one person can do that! We need to give them some space to work on their own recovery without our constant intervention. They will need our support and love during this time. They will also need other significant relationships to help them recover. We need to let go and get as many of our needs met through our relationship with God and through our relationship with other disciples. A great goal, as Paul teaches in Philippians 4:11-13, is to become content and at peace with yourself and your circumstances. The alcoholic must strive to be at peace not using. The codependent needs to strive to be at peace with his or her relationship with God and the grace he has been given. As Paul learned when he pleaded to have his thorn removed, God said, "My grace is sufficient for you, for my power is made perfect in weakness" (2 Corinthians 12:9).

One of the most enlightening lessons for me was when I learned that it was not my responsibility to make my husband happy. To be happy or not was his choice. My actions are meant to bring him happiness, but ultimately if he decides to be sad, angry or distant, it is still his choice. I should not take it on as my responsibility to try to change him. What a relief that was! My constant effort to alter my husband's moods was like rolling a boulder up Mt. Everest! It just didn't happen, no matter how hard I tried.

Our spouses can no longer be our gods, consume all our thoughts, be our reasons for living, or our barometers of how much we are loved. It is God who ultimately loves us and has given us his purpose. It is on this that we must build our self-esteem, our love for ourselves and our love for others. Good deeds or sin do not change God's level of love for us. He loves us because he created us!

Forgiveness

Just what is forgiveness anyway? How exactly do you turn intense bitterness, rage and hatred into unconditional love? To me, it was like moving a mountain, but by following four simple steps, it broke down the walls I so firmly erected around my heart.

Step 1: Forgiveness means "to grant pardon without harboring resentment." To grant pardon it is often necessary to go back and look at how much God has had to forgive you. Go ahead—get that scroll out. List them all. If you're stuck, read Galatians 5:19-21, 2 Timothy 3:1-5 and Mark 7:20-23 for some help. Look at what Jesus says concerning forgiveness in Matthew 6:14-15:

> "For if you forgive men when they sin against you, your heavenly Father will also forgive you. But if

you do not forgive men their sins, your Father will
not forgive your sins."

There is a high cost if you do not forgive those who hurt
you. As they have hurt you, so your scroll of sin is a testi-
mony of how you have hurt God. You are not so different
from the alcoholic (Matthew 7:3). All sin is sin against God
and in many instances, when you break it all down, you are
often guilty of the same amount of sin.

Step 2: Read Luke 6:32-38 and identify how bitterness
and rage for your spouse affects and inhibits your own relationship with God. God sees everyone's sin as the same. As
you may have heard it said, "The ground is level at the foot
of the cross." God's love means giving even when we receive
nothing in return. That's what makes it "unconditional" love.
We, as disciples, give in love, because it pleases God.

Step 3: Pray deeply that God will change your heart as
in Psalm 51. Write a forgiveness letter to your spouse or
talk to him about your part in the destruction of your relationship. Treat your spouse with a genuine level of forgiveness that you've never shown before. You may be the only
Bible he ever reads, the only Jesus he ever gets to see. Be a
true ambassador of Jesus in your home.

Step 4: Once you have forgiven your spouse, you need
to forget as God does. In Hebrews 8:12 he says, "for I will
forgive their wickedness and will remember their sins no
more." God acknowledges that what was done against him
was wicked, yet his forgiveness is complete. No holding on
or rehearsing the "remember when's." Jesus looked at the
wickedness of others and said, "They know not what they
do" (Luke 23:34). In the same way, we need to see that the

alcoholic truly does not understand what he is doing or what he has done to you. Your change of heart allows God to work through you to offer your spouse the mercy and grace he needs.

Overcoming Critical Attitudes

Another key to firmly establishing your recovery is in abolishing critical attitudes. One excellent lesson my friend Debbie Wright taught me was to "sweep my own side of the street." Stop looking at the leaves in the gutter on the other person's side. I needed to keep my focus on my own righteousness, since there is plenty of work to do there!

In John 8:1-11 you see Jesus talking to those accusing the woman caught in adultery. He makes them look at themselves. Why? Because Jesus believes in forgiveness, not stoning. Ask yourself: Do I treat my spouse with grace, speaking the truth in love, or do I stone him? Stoning kills relationships. Grace leads to repentance and renewed life. Jesus doesn't want people condemned. He wants everyone to feel the tremendous power of his grace. And it is that feeling of grace that motivates us toward lasting change. So when you find yourself in a critical mode, focus on the person's positive attributes (Philippians 4:8). Florence Schachinger taught me to make a list of my husband's best qualities, memorize it, then to mention at least two every day to build him up. Remember, women, what Proverbs 31:12 says, "She brings him good, not harm, all the days of her life."

Pure Motivations

You need to rebuild your foundation on Jesus, even if your spouse does not enter recovery or respond to your changes. Your repentance of the sin of codependency must be motivated by your love for Christ and not by a scheme to make your spouse go into a detox program or become a

Christian. Recovery from codependency does not ensure that your spouse will become a Christian. Your spouse's decision to follow God or to recover is his alone. The Bible says he "may be won over without words by the purity and reverence of your life" (1 Peter 3:1-2). It does not say he *will* be. Remember, at the end of your life you will stand before God alone, without your spouse. Jesus was the one willing to lay down his life for you, and willingly you must lay down your life for him.

Remember recovery takes place one day at a time. It will happen. You will get better. And remember, God is always with you to see you through to victory!

The Resurrected Life

> Jesus said to her, "I am the resurrection and the life. He who believes in me will live, even though he dies; and whoever lives and believes in me will never die" (John 11:25-26).

When you have overcome powerlessness with Jesus, when you tell the whole truth, when you write and read your journal and surrender control of your life to God, when you implement your plan to avoid rescuing and rebuild your foundation on Jesus, the result is a resurrected life. It will be a life very different from the one you are living now. People will see your joy and will wonder: "Is it really Jesus that changed her, as she says?" And you can share with them your faith in the miracle of recovery that Jesus has performed in you!

My prayer for you, like Peter's, is that:

> In this you greatly rejoice, though now for a little while you may have had to suffer grief in all kinds of trials. These have come so that your faith—of greater worth than gold, which perishes even

though refined by fire—may be proved genuine and may result in praise, glory and honor when Jesus Christ is revealed. Though you have not seen him, you love him; and even though you do not see him now, you believe in him and are filled with an inexpressible and glorious joy, for you are receiving the goal of your faith, the salvation of your souls (1 Peter 1:6-9).

10

B R E N D A   L E A T H E R W O O D

My Husband Stopped Drinking
So Why Am I So Unhappy?

A couple of years ago, I was talking to a beautiful young woman whose husband had recently graduated from our chemical recovery ministry. He was doing great! He was happy, fruitful, respected by his peers, very successful in his new job and a patient, loving husband and father. She, however, was depressed, angry and had stopped coming to church. When her husband had been using or was in the earlier stages of his recovery, she had felt a sense of purpose and strength. She had been determined to fight for her husband's soul and had been very instrumental in his recovery. Now she explained to me, she no longer felt needed. Her husband had taken over much of what had been her responsibility, including their finances and his part in training and disciplining their son.

As I listened to her, I realized that she had done all she knew to do, and now felt let down because she did not know how to be a godly wife to someone who was doing well spiritually. This was all new to her. She had always been the wife of someone who was deceitful, manipulative and struggling spiritually. All of her training as a young Christian had been on how to be a good wife to this kind of husband. Now that God had answered her prayer in giving

her the husband she dreamed of, she was totally unprepared, frustrated and discouraged.

The Reality of Recovery

What she needed was to be taught from the Scriptures
how to have a great marriage with a husband who was also
a disciple. We talked about stepping into a new role, about
letting her husband become the leader in their home. We
discussed the effect that would have on her everyday life,
and what needs he now had that only she could fill. I watched
the life come back into her, and since that day she has continued to grow into a powerful woman and an incredibly
happy wife and mother. I learned that day how important it
is to not only undo the old patterns of sin, but also to teach
what the Bible says about forming new patterns of godli-
ness, in this case, the way to have a happy marriage.

For those of us blessed by God with husbands who are
recovering, the initial response to their recovery is relief,
incredible joy and high hopes for an exciting and productive future. Unfortunately, Satan only departs for a short
time, and then comes back with a new plan to destroy our
joy and hope. It would be foolish to think that just because
our husband, wife, parent, child or friend has stopped using, we will be able to stand undaunted by whatever attacks
Satan may wage against us.

When Mike and I lived in Louisville, Kentucky, I attended a series of classes for "Concerned Persons" at the
Jefferson Alcohol and Drug Abuse Center. One of the most
alarming things I learned there was that most marriages break
up *after* the spouse with the chemical addiction recovers. I
remember thinking how sad it was that a wife or husband
could go through years of pain while his or her spouse was
using, and then during recovery, the spouse let their marriage fall apart. Like many of us who are not touched per-

sonally by addiction, or who don't know yet that we are touched personally by addiction, I was being very smug and self-righteous. I thought that simply because they were not disciples, they did not know how to deal with life. When it happened in my own life, however, I learned how wrong I was. I saw firsthand how crafty Satan is and how dangerous it is to be unprepared for his attacks. It is my hope that sharing my experience will help many of you to experience the joy of living with someone who is recovering.

Mike and I were married in 1973. I came from a family of teetotalers and assumed that everyone from "the traditional church" held to that same philosophy. However, after we were married, Mike told me that he drank a glass of wine from time to time and that it was not wrong to do so. I was surprised, but not alarmed, and occasionally I had a glass with him. I first remember seeing my husband drunk in 1978. He came home late and was slurring his words. He could hardly walk and was giggling at himself like a schoolgirl. I was horrified. Later he told me that he had taken too much of a prescription cold medicine, and I was all too happy to believe him. He assured me that it would never happen again and it didn't—for a while.

As time went on, however, there were unmistakable signs that things were not right. There were gaps of time missing and unaccounted for. There were times when he came to bed hours after I had fallen asleep smelling like alcohol. There were times when he was violently sick and throwing up (hungover). Then there were the bottles. I began to find empty bottles in the trunk of our car, in our trash and in our basement. Whenever I asked about any of these things, however, I was eager to believe whatever flimsy excuse Mike would offer. I could not imagine what my life would be like if my husband had a serious problem with alcohol, so I simply refused to see what was right in front of my face.

When we moved to New York in 1985, things improved tremendously for several months. But, like any worldly attempt at recovery other than repentance, the problems soon reappeared. As Lisa Johnson discipled me in my marriage, I learned to tell the truth about what I saw and feared. As the truth came out, my husband humbly and sincerely repented and was baptized as a disciple. God had given me the husband I had always wanted and believed that Mike could be.

Although many of the problems associated with drinking did disappear when Mike recovered, there were other things in our lives that had to change before real healing could take place in our marriage. During the fifteen years we had been married, I had made many adjustments to his abuse, that is, I compensated for his weaknesses. I had taken over the leadership role in our home. Although Mike's drinking was a subject we never discussed, it was a very real presence and influence in our home.

I heard an illustration once which compared living with an alcoholic to living with an elephant in your living room. The family being described never actually acknowledged its existence, but it was very much there. They learned to walk around it, ignore its mess, rearrange the furniture so they could see the TV over it, etc. As time went by, the children grew up and began to realize that not everyone had an elephant in their living room. They wondered why they had to put up with this inconvenience all those years. Some of the kids became resentful of the parents for not dealing with it, while others continued to ignore it. At any rate, every family member was affected by it, and made adjustments in their lives to deal with its presence.

In order to provide a healthy home atmosphere to help Mike recover in, I had to undo many of the sinful adjustments I had made over the years to his drinking. Joanne Randall has done a great job defining the sins involved in codependency. When you are in the middle of the situation, however, they are very hard to see. The addict's sins are obvious and as a result, the spouse can look very noble and good. It is very important that the husband or wife gets the opportunity to see and repent of his or her sins so that refreshing from God can come to them, as well, and they can take part in the healing process that must occur for the addict to recover and the home to be happy.

When Mike stopped drinking, I remember an overwhelming sense of guilt. I talked to Lisa about it often in our discipling times, but I was never clear as to why I was feeling so guilty. I remember Lisa asking me if there was anything that I had not told her, thinking perhaps, that there was some secret sin in my life. There was secret sin all right, but it was a secret from me, too. I had made adjustments to our life-style that were completely sinful, but in my mind they were necessary.

For example, because of my husband's drinking problem, I was often disappointed by promises he would make and not keep. I did not deal with this in a godly manner. Instead, I learned to not depend on him for anything. I became very independent and distant. If I didn't need him, he couldn't hurt me. This is what I call a sinful adjustment to a sinful situation. There were many such adjustments in my life, and I needed to repent of them all. The problem was that I did not see them. As a result, I did not repent, and my sin continued to destroy our family's happiness, even though Mike was no longer drinking. Looking back on these times, I appreciate even more Mike's determination to recover, because I know that I did not make it easy for him.

Satan's Arsenal Against the Codependent

It is the failure of the codependent spouse to see his sin and repent that causes so many marriages to break up after the addicted husband or wife stops drinking or using. I thank God that there were people in my life who helped me through those hard times. Even though they knew nothing about "codependency" at the time, they knew about sin and helped me repent each time my sin showed its ugly face.

Below are just a few of the sins that Satan has used in my life, especially during the early days of Mike's recovery. Expect Satan to use them in your life. Please keep in mind that I am talking to the spouse of a recovering alcoholic or drug addict.

Fear

One of Satan's most effective weapons is fear. For the person who has lived for years with an alcoholic or drug addict, there is a lot of pain and hurt. The idea of trusting this person again with your emotions, your finances, your children and your life can be frightening. I was never afraid of Mike hurting me physically, but the emotional pain was very destructive. For codependent people there are a lot of risks when they decide to trust the recovering person again. They are, in essence, giving the spouse back the power to hurt them. Thoughts of doubt and mistrust flood their minds. "Can I really trust you now?" "If I give you back your role in our family, will you let me down again?" "What will I do if you mess up our finances? I am afraid to let go of the little bit of control I do have."

The Bible is our sword, the only weapon we have with which to fight Satan's schemes. The only solutions for our fears are in the Word. 1 Peter 3:1-6, 13-14; 1 John 4:18 and 1 Corinthians 10:13 are great for dealing with fear. We must learn to go to the Word for the strength to fight the fear Satan sends our way.

Pride

Pride may very well be even more powerful than fear. In our pride we defend ourselves at all costs. We put up walls to protect our hearts, our ego and our confidence. "I want to keep control over our finances, children, and schedule. I don't need you. I have done it alone all these years, and we are fine the way we are. Just fix yourself. You're the problem."

Resentment, the sister sin of pride, says, *"Who do you think you are to come in here and try to take over after the way you've hurt us all these years?"*

We excuse ourselves because of our spouse's addiction, and in our pride we set ourselves above the law of God, which clearly states, "Submit to one another out of reverence for Christ" (Ephesians 5:21). Wives, whatever your situation may be, the Bible still says to you what it says to everyone else: "Wives, submit to your husbands as to the Lord. For the husband is the head of the wife as Christ is the head of the church..." (Ephesians 5:22-23). If your husband or wife sincerely repents and begins recovery, it is only right to help him or her back into the role that God has planned for him or her. This is the only way the family can function properly and be happy. Anything else is a spiritual maladjustment.

Bitterness

Bitterness is another of Satan's favorite weapons. Bitterness says, "You may be on your white horse now, but I remember who you've been, and I'll never forget what you've done to me. How dare you try to fix me! I'm not the one who threw our money away on drugs and alcohol!" Bitterness springs from an unforgiving heart. No heart is happy when it is unforgiving and bitter.

The Bible's teaching on the importance of forgiveness is clear. In Matthew 6:15, Jesus says that if we do not forgive those who sin against us, God will not forgive us our sins. 1 Corinthians 13:5 says that "love keeps no record of wrongs." Whatever happens, whatever we decide to do, we must never allow bitterness to take root, but do all we can to help each other repent with a spirit of forgiveness (Hebrews 12:15).

Deceit

Of all Satan's weapons, perhaps the most difficult to see is the sin of not loving the truth. Certainly the truth is not always pleasant, but Jesus always told us the truth. Satan is the father of lies. We need to love the truth because it is the language of God, and all deceit is the native language of the devil (John 8:44). The trouble with codependency is that it is built on lies. We hate the truth so much, that we create a false world where no one ever hurts us. We eagerly believe the lies of those we love who are abusing alcohol or other drugs. We believe them because it is easy and comforting. The truth is hard to deal with and requires courage and faith. As we help the recovering person, we must be honest with him about what we see, what we fear and what we know. If we think he is drinking or using drugs again, we must say so because it is the truth. We must make a decision to put off all falsehood and speak the truth in love to one another (Ephesians 4:15, 25; Colossians 3:9).

There are many other sins that could be listed here, but these are some of the ones most commonly found in the lives of codependent spouses. Learning to identify the sin as sin may sound simple, but it is difficult to those who have focused their lives on the sins of others and felt justified in their own. Identifying sin as sin is the first step in repentance, which is so important not only in rebuilding broken lives, but also for the salvation of our souls.

Of course, codependency doesn't just apply to the husband-wife relationship. There are families torn apart by sons and daughters, children deeply scarred by their parents, and many other relationships affected by the nightmare of chemical addiction and codependency. These principles are presented in the marriage situation, because this is a common example of the type of relationship in which they occur and because this is the way I first experienced them. It is our hope that these principles and scriptures will be helpful in whatever situation you need to apply them.[1]

Possible Relapse

What if my husband relapses? Although Mike has not had a drink in almost ten years, I have never forgotten that this is a very real possibility. Satan had this foothold in my husband's life for twenty years. He did not easily give it up.

For some, relapse is a part of recovery. Not everyone who eventually recovers stops and never picks up or takes a drink one more time. Of course, this is what we all hope for and pray will happen, but it is not always the way it works. Some people do get drunk or high again after they repent. Does this mean they did not repent? Think about this! What did you repent of when you became a Christian? Lying, fits of rage, jealousy? Have you fallen into these sins again since becoming a Christian? If so, does it mean you did not repent? No! Repentance means change, but it does not mean perfection. For the person recovering from drug or alcohol addiction, repentance is no different.

One reason we have the CR groups, and not groups for lying, greed, hate and so on, is because returning to this sin can be life-threatening, while returning to the others is usually not. I have seen many relapse and still go on to recover. I have also seen others who relapsed and died in detox units. One friend of ours fell off a bridge and became severely brain damaged. Mike has already mentioned a friend who was murdered while in relapse. We have known several who attempted suicide under the influence of drugs and alcohol. Relapse is a dangerous thing, but it is not necessarily an indication that the person you love is not serious or is not going to recover eventually.

So, how can you know when someone is serious? As has been said many times already in this book, believe what he does, not what he says. When Mike repented, he was told to read his journal first to his discipleship group and then to our entire church staff. He did. He was told to take his discipling partner and me through our house and show us all the places he had hidden alcohol. He did. He was told that he could not be alone for six months. He had to be with an adult every minute. He could not get in the car and drive to the store, and he could not stay home with the kids while I went out. We had to go together. Whatever he was doing, he had to work around my schedule. If I had a Bible study or counseling session, I had to drop him off at someone's house, or he had to go with me. He had to go to bed when I wanted to go. He did all of this, and he never complained. He was willing to do anything to recover. He took all the advice he got and did it exactly as he was advised to do it. His attitude was always, "I don't deserve to be trusted. I need to win back your trust and respect." And he did.

What does this all mean? What if my husband or father or wife or son is doing what he or she is told, but he is complaining or feels it is unfair? What if I see him changing the advice just a little? What if he is late? People give warning signs that they are going to drink before they do. All of these are indications that they are not motivated to recover. They may be mad that they cannot drink or use drugs. They have not surrendered to the fact that they cannot predict the outcome if they take one drink, or one toke, or one hit, etc. They may have surrendered, but are slipping back into denial and what is known in AA circles as "stinkin' thinking."

Anger and depression are to be expected to an extent. Giving up their drug of choice is like losing their best friend, and sometimes they have to go through a grieving process. The steps to acceptance include denial, bargaining, anger and depression, but they need to be talking about these feelings in their CR group or to their own discipling partner.[2] You can never feel sorry for them, or get hooked into their self-pity. Remember, the only way they can get their lives back is to stop drinking or doing drugs. Look for gratitude. This is the key. They should be so grateful to God to be alive and grateful to the people who are willing to invest in them that they do not give in to feelings of "Poor me," or "This is too hard." Mike's attitude was "I'll do anything. I'll go to any lengths to recover." This is the only attitude that leads to recovery. All others lead to relapse.

I recently spoke to another young woman who did a formal intervention with her husband almost six months ago. He went into treatment. Things had gone fairly well, but there were some things she did not feel good about. For example, he still went to bars and hung out with his drinking buddies, even though he had been advised not to. He felt he could handle it. He stopped going to his aftercare counselor, and he had only gone to two AA meetings in the five months since he got out of treatment. His attitude was not one of gratitude, and he complained a lot about how much was expected of him. She knew these were indications of relapse.

She called me a few days ago and told me she had found

drugs in their home. When she confronted him, he told her that he was keeping it "for a friend." But she did not believe him. He gave her many excuses for his behavior, but she did not accept any of them. She knew that his continued drug use was threatening to destroy their marriage, so she did not give in to the temptation to look the other way or to believe his excuses. She listened to what he had been doing and not to what he said. This is the only hope her husband had for recovery. She said to me, "I believe that losing me would be his bottom, and I am willing to do anything to help him hit bottom. I still believe he has a lot to give to God's kingdom, and I am not giving up." This is real love, tough love. It's tough for her and tough for him. This is love that exudes faith and hope. This is a courageous love. This is God's love.

When the ones we love begin recovering, we cannot take a vacation from our own spiritual growth. While we and the angels in heaven are rejoicing, we need to remember that the lion never sleeps. He is still roaming around looking for someone to devour (1 Peter 5:8). As Mike Taliaferro states in his book, *The Lion Never Sleeps,*

> The lion is coming.... He cannot be bought, bribed, bargained with or deterred. No man can outrun him. He studies every weakness. And he will attack with fury and with an intent to kill.[3]

This is the bad news, but the good news is that we can be prepared for him. We are engaged in a spiritual battle for the rest of our lives, but with our God we can always win. We will never face any temptation from which God has not already provided a way for us to escape (1 Corinthians 10:13). Together we can win against the attack of chemical addiction in the lives of those we love.[4]

11

MIKE LEATHERWOOD

Starting a Chemical Recovery Group

L et me begin with some good news. You can have an effective chemical recovery ministry without spending a dime. For eleven years, Brenda and I oversaw the CR ministry, raised up leaders and started twenty-five new CR groups while either leading a significant church ministry or working full-time with HOPE *worldwide*. This should be good news for church leaders and administrators.

Selecting Leaders

The most important part of getting started is to select the right leaders. Like any other ministry, the CR ministry will only be as good as the people who lead it. I would encourage you to select one couple to be in charge and another couple to assist them. Since you will be dividing into men and women's groups, it is important to have good leaders for both the men and the women.

It is not necessary for the person you select to be recovering from drugs and alcohol. Although this might be helpful, it is definitely not the most important quality. Here is a short list of the most important things to look for:

1. The candidates need to be doing well spiritually.

2. They need to have the confidence of the lead evangelist and women's ministry leader. It helps if they are
   in the discipleship group with the main leaders.
3. The chemical recovery leaders need to be perceptive
   and have good insight into people.
4. They need to be evangelistically fruitful.
5. They need to have a desire and a vision for this ministry. Just being willing to do it is not enough.

If you are a leader reading this list, you are probably
thinking that if you had people with these qualifications
they would be leading a significant portion of your church,
but that is just my point. Brenda and I were in the full-
time ministry when Steve and Lisa Johnson asked us to
start the CR ministry. You can do it with full-time people
who are already in the ministry, if they have a real heart
for it. In fact, it would probably be better to wait in starting your CR ministry if you don't feel that you have the
people on staff that it would take to make it great. I know
Steve and Lisa believe the investment has been worth it in
New York. One suggestion, however, if you really feel
stretched right now is to have a full-time couple oversee
the ministry, and disciple another couple who would be
the "hands-on" leaders. The full-time couple should attend the groups periodically.

Having an excellent assistant couple is important for at
least two reasons. First, since many of the people in your
groups are still experiencing some denial, we need other
people to help us break through their defenses. Second, it is
very easy for us to lose our objectivity or "get hooked" by
our own fears, sentimentality or prejudices. For example, I
always need to have someone assisting me when there are
older men in the group. My southern upbringing makes it
difficult for me to be as honest and straightforward as I need

to be. The people who "hook" you may be different, but the fact is that we all get hooked and need the objectivity of other eyes and ears.

One of my goals early in the ministry was to inspire and raise up other leaders. I knew that as the church grew, so would the number of disciples who would need the CR group. Almost every week, I spent time giving people a vision for being able to lead other groups. Today, many of our current leaders were a part of those early groups. It is exciting to see people who have felt worthless catch a dream and nurture it into reality. This training has also helped prepare many of these people for other leadership roles in the kingdom.

Group Members

Because you will be trying to accomplish a number of things in your first group, you should plan to have a variety of people attend. For example, if your church has several hundred members, then you already have dozens of people who could benefit from the group. It also means that you will need to begin to train people in different sectors to lead groups as soon as possible. Probably the best way to select the recovering people who should attend is to look for the most motivated. To determine that, you may need to have a personal interview with those people recommended by a sector leader.

My suggestion is to start one group for men and another for women. Select two people to train from two other sectors. After your interviews choose four of the most motivated people who need the group and have them attend with their discipling partners. This makes ten people, plus you and the assistant, which makes twelve. Remember your first group needs to be of high quality. Nothing will build this group's confidence like victory!

Format of the Group

Your group should meet in a neat, clean, bright environment (which may preclude some single brothers' households!) The meeting lasts ninety minutes. We must absolutely start on time and not go overtime. Here is the suggested format for the group.

1. Start with a short, spiritual, upbeat devotional (ten minutes).
2. Have a time of good news sharing. Having good news to share is very important to recovery. It means we are staying in touch with God's blessings (ten minutes).
3. The remainder of the time will be used for issues such as journal reading or dealing with a relapse. New members in the group are asked to begin writing their journal right away.[1] Sometimes I will lead a discussion on a topic related to recovery, for example, powerlessness, serenity, going to any lengths, surrender or relapse.

Group Dynamics

Feedback is expected during appropriate times. People in the group need to be confrontational and direct, but everyone is required to make their comments with genuine concern. People are taught to speak the truth in love (Ephesians 4:15) and to make their comments in the first person in order to avoid sounding "preachy." For example, a comment on someone's journal might go something like this:

> "John, I heard you say that you believe you're powerless over crack cocaine, but that you still believe that you can drink alcohol. I want you to know that what you said scares me for you, because I know when I've felt like that in the past, using alcohol always took me back to my drug of choice."

The first time people attend, we ask them to just listen. Comments by group members need to help the person connect the pain with using drugs. It is pain that humbles a person and motivates him to get help. Failure to get honest in connecting with the pain or justifying, rationalizing, glamorizing and blame-shifting his or her drug use are all signs of a lack of motivation to recover. Remember, you can only help people who are sick and tired of being sick and tired. Assessing motivation by what people do is the only way to invest in the people who really want to change.

This is the reason we continue to remind both the recovering person and his or her discipling partner that being on time for chemical recovery group is so important. It is an indication of one's desire to get better. This isn't done in a harsh way, but in a firm, no-nonsense way which really helps the alcoholic know that he is going to be held accountable for what he does.

Remember that the CR group is a program of spiritual recovery sponsored by the church. It is not meant to take the place of a formal treatment program for those who need it. Our group leaders are not, for the most part, certified substance abuse counselors. They are members of the church who have been trained to help people recover spiritually from the ravages of drug addiction. Keep it spiritual, and keep it simple.

Periodically, we have to ask a person to leave the group because of a lack of motivation. These people are always discharged with a "contract." This is a simple, clear and verbal understanding of what it will take for them to get back into the group. This contract must be fulfilled completely before a person can come back.

Sometimes people decide that they don't need to be in the CR group. The sector leader should be called and the situation should be explained. This is another good reason for having the discipling partner at each group.

There are times when people use drugs or drink, even though they are attending CR group. This may be an indication that they need more focus on recovery than a weekly group provides. We usually have that person begin to attend one or two AA meetings a week with one of the older Christians or his discipling partner. If they have another slip and use, but seem very determined to repent and stay sober, then they may need to attend additional AA meetings, be referred to a detox unit for a few days or even to an inpatient program for twenty-eight to thirty days, depending on the frequency and severity.[2] An attitude of humility and a willingness to go to any lengths is the determining factor in whether you can help this person.

If continued drunkenness occurs, coupled with an argumentative and resistant attitude, then the Bible leaves us no recourse but to withdraw our fellowship in hopes that this will help him to hit bottom and come back to God (1 Corinthians 5: 9-11). This is a decision that should be made by your elders.

Graduation from CR

After a person writes a successful journal, listens to several other journals and attends three lectures on spiritual recovery, they become a candidate for graduation. The leader of the group talks to the discipling partner and the assistant leader in order to determine if the candidate, in addition to fulfilling the requirements of CR, is doing well spiritually. If so, then he is recommended for graduation.

Informal graduations are held in the group. Everyone gets a chance to share with the graduate and then he gets to share with them. Formal graduations are held quarterly. All the current CR members and leaders come together for a time of celebration. Family and friends are invited. For some people, this is the first thing they have ever completed in their lives, so it is very special. We have some great entertainment, and then we bring the graduates up front with their group to share. It is incredibly moving to see the power of God at work, literally transforming lives before our eyes.

On New Year's Eve we have a special party in honor of all those who have enjoyed a year or more of continuous sobriety. It is an awesome party, and a sober way to see in the New Year. What an incredible blessing to see so many who were previously enslaved to alcohol or other drugs experience the power and forgiveness of God, to see their chains broken away, to see their lives and souls literally restored!

Appendix

Available Resources

Al-Anon Family Groups
Headquarters
1392 Broadway
New York, NY 10018-0862
Phone: (212) 302-7240

Alateen
1372 Broadway
New York, NY 10018-0862
Phone: (212) 302-7240

Alcoholics Anonymous
P.O. Box 459
Grand Central Station
New York, NY 10017

Hazelden Foundation
P.O. Box 11
Center City, MN 55012
Phone: 1-800-257-7800
(For a free catalog of books
and tapes, call toll free.)

Johnson Institute
7151 Metro Blvd.
Minneapolis, MN 55435
Phone: 1-800-231-5165

National Clearinghouse for
Alcohol/Drug Information
P.O. Box 2345
Rockville, MD 20852
Phone: (301) 468-2600

National Coalition for the
Prevention of Drug and
Alcohol Abuse
537 Jones Road
Greenville, Ohio 43023
Phone: (614) 587-2800

National Council
on Alcoholism, Inc. (NCA)
12 West 21st Street, 7th Floor
New York, NY 10010
Phone: 1-800-NCA-CALL

National Institute
on Alcohol Abuse
and Alcoholism (NIAAA)
Parklawn Bldg.,
Room 16-105
5600 Fishers Lane
Rockville, MD 20857
Phone: (301) 443-3885

Notes

Chapter 1—Defining Chemical Dependency

1. Father Joseph C. Martin, *No Laughing Matter* (New York: Harper & Row, 1982), 5.

2. These figures are taken from a series of lectures entitled "Chalk Talks" which were delivered at the Jefferson Alcohol and Drug Abuse Center, Louisville, Ky., 1985.

3. For an excellent history of Alcoholics Anonymous and its impact on the alcoholic in the U.S., see *Alcoholics Anonymous Comes of Age* (New York: Alcoholics Anonymous Publishing Co., 1957).

4. See Chapter 4, "Disciples and Alcohol."

5. Vernon E. Johnson, "Rational Defense and Projection," *I'll Quit Tomorrow* (New York: Harper Collins Publishers, 1980), 27-34.

6. Howard J. Clinebell, *Understanding and Counseling the Alcoholic* (Nashville: Abingdon Press, 1968), 21.

7. E.M. Jellinek, *The Disease Concept of Alcoholism* (New Haven: College and University Press in association with Hillhouse Press, New Brunswick, N.J., 1960), 36-41.

8. William Leipold, "What Protects Me (Defenses)?", *Walk Through the Valley* (Independence, Mo.: Independence Press, 1975), 70-85.

9. Father Joseph C. Martin, "Alcoholism is Addiction to a Drug," *No Laughing Matter*, 85-93.

10. *Alcoholics Anonymous* (New York: AA World Services, Inc., 1939), 60-63.

11. "Tobacco, Alcohol and Illicit Drug Deaths," *NY State Office of Alcohol and Substance Abuse Services*, June 19, 1995, 32-37.

12. Tom Jones, *Mind Change: The Overcomer's Handbook* (Woburn, Mass.: Discipleship Publications International, 1994).

13. E.M. Jellinek's chart is modified and explained by John E. Keller, *Ministering to Alcoholics* (Minneapolis: Augsbury Press, 1966), 24-34.

Chapter 2—Converting the Addict

1. David Wilmes, "Facts About Kids' Use of Alcohol and Other Drugs," *Parenting for Prevention* (Minneapolis: Johnson Institute, 1995), 31-33. The entire chapter has a wealth of up-to-date information on juvenile use of inhalants and other drugs.

2. *Alcoholics Anonymous*, 58-59.

3. For an excellent explanation of the difference between surrender and compliance, see Harry S. Tiebout, "Surrender Versus Compliance in Therapy with Special Reference to Alcoholism," *Quarterly Journal of Studies on Alcoholism*, 14 (March 1953): 59. This is now part of series of articles by Harry Tiebout available from the Hazelden Foundation. (See Bibliography.)

4. This illustration was used during a family therapy group called "Concerned Persons" conducted by the Jefferson Alcohol and Drug Abuse Center, Louisville, Ky. 1985.

5. Leipold, *Walk Through the Valley*, 70-85.

Chapter 3—Discipling the Addict

1. Al Baird, "Takin' It Higher," *L.A. Story*, Volume 3, Issue 10, August 18, 1996.

2. Although David Wilmes' book deals specifically with prevention, there is a very helpful section explaining HALT, *Parenting for Prevention*, 169-172.

3. Terence T. Gorski, "Counseling for Relapse Prevention," taken from a one-day skills training workshop. The CENAPS Corporation, Homeward, Ill., 1986 and Charles Crew, *A Look at Relapse* (Center City, Minn.: Hazelden Foundation, 1974), 3-10.

4. Elizabeth Kubler-Ross, *On Death and Dying* (New York: Collier Books, 1969), 34-121.

Chapter 4—Disciples and Alcohol

1. "Brain Images of Addiction Show the Neural Basis of Drug Cravings," *New York Times*, Aug. 13, 1996, sec. C, 1.

Chapter 5—No More Playing God

1. Ernst Kurtz, *Not God* (Center City, Minn.: Hazelden Foundation, 1969).

2. Clinebell, "What Is An Alcoholic?", *Understanding and Counseling the Alcoholic*, 17-41.

3. For an excellent treatment of these concepts and to spiritually prepare you to work with people both in and out of recovery, see Gordon Ferguson, *Victory of Surrender* (Woburn, Mass.: Discipleship Publications International, 1995).

Chapter 6—Intervention

1. John and Pat O'Neill, *Concerned Intervention,* and Vernon E. Johnson, *Intervention* (Minneapolis, Minn.: Johnson Institute, 1986), and Roque Fajardo, *Helping Your Alcoholic Before He or She Hits Bottom* (New York: Crown Publishers, 1976).

Chapter 7—Approaches to Treatment

1. This is an essential work for anyone who is serious about understanding the mind of the alcoholic.

2. *Alcoholics Anonymous Comes of Age*, 276.

3. John and Pat O'Neill, *Concerned Intervention* (Oakland, Ca.: New Harbinger Publications, Inc., 1992), 137-138.

4. How to write a journal is discussed in Chapter 1, "Defining Chemical Dependency."

Chapter 9—Codependency Recovery

1. I am indebted to Jan Silvious whose book, *Please Don't Say You Need Me,* first introduced me to this idea (Grand Rapids, Mich.: Zondervan Publications, 1989), 151.

2. Jerry Bridges, *Trusting God Even When Life Hurts* (Colorado Springs: Navpress, 1988).

3. Gordon Ferguson, *The Victory of Surrender* (Woburn, Mass.: Discipleship Publications International, 1995).

4. Al J. Mooney, *The Recovery Book* (New York: Workman Publishers Inc., 1992), 510.

5. Sam and Geri Laing, *Friends and Lovers* (Woburn, Mass.: Discipleship Publications International, 1996), 68.

Chapter 10—My Husband Stopped Drinking

1. For parents who suspect that their child may be using, or for information and guidelines on prevention, please read Beth Polson and Miller Newton, Ph. D., *Not My Kid: A Parent's Guide to Kids and Drugs* (New York: Avon Books, 1985) and David J. Wilmes, *Parenting for Prevention: How to Raise a Child to Say No to Alcohol/Drugs* (Minneapolis: Johnson Institute, 1995).

2. Elisabeth Kubler-Ross, *On Death and Dying*, 34-121.

3. Mike Taliaferro, *The Lion Never Sleeps* (Woburn, Mass.: Discipleship Publications International, 1996), 46.

4. A number of other books which will be helpful in studying this subject further are John E. Keller, *Counseling the Spouse, Ministering to Alcoholics*, 124-137., Celia Dulfano, *Families, Alcoholism and Recovery* (Minneapolis: Hazelden Foundation, 1982), and Howard J. Clinebell, "Helping the Family of the Alcoholic," *Understanding and Counseling the Alcoholic*, 266-293. If you have teens in your home who are addicted to drugs, or who you suspect are using, many of these principles will apply. However, dealing with adolescent drug use can be tricky. I would suggest reading Beth Polson and Miller Newton, *Not My Kid* (New York: Avon Books, 1984), Dick Schaffer, *Choices and Consequences* (Minneapolis, Minn.: Johnson Institute, 1987), and David Wilmes, *Parenting for Prevention*.

Chapter 11—Starting a Chemical Recovery Group

1. For a detailed discussion on how to write a journal, see Chapter 2, "Converting the Addict." Additional information on how our chemical recovery groups function can be found in the Chapter 5, "Playing God."

2. See Chapter 7, "Approaches to Treatment."

Bibliography

Alcoholics Anonymous, AA World Services, Inc. New York: 1939.

Alcoholics Anonymous Comes of Age, Alcoholics Anonymous Publishing Inc., 1957.

Black, Claudia, Ph.D., M.S.W. *It Will Never Happen to Me*. New York: Ballentine Books, 1981.

Bridges, Jerry. *Trusting God: Even When Life Hurts*. Colorado Springs, Colo.: Navpress, 1988.

Clinebell, Harold J. *Understanding and Counseling the Alcoholic*. Nashville: Abingdon Press, 1968.

Crew, Charles. *A Look at Relapse*. Center City, Minn.: Hazelden Foundation, 1974.

Dulfano, Celia. *Families, Alcoholism and Recovery*. Center City, Minn.: Hazelden Foundation, 1982.

Ferguson, Gordon. *The Victory of Surrender*. Woburn, Mass.: Discipleship Publications International, 1995.

Fajardo, Rogue. *Helping Your Alcoholic Before He or She Hits Bottom*. New York: Crown Publishers, 1976.

Goleman, Daniel. "Brain Images of Addiction Show the New Basis of Drug Cravings." *New York Times*, August 13,1996, Sec. C,1.

Gorski, Terence T. *Counseling for Relapse Prevention*. Homeward, Ill.: The CENAPS Corporation, 1986.

Denial Patterns: A System for Understanding the Alcoholic's Behavior. Hazel Crest, Ill.: The CENAPS Corp., 1976.

Jellineck, E.M. *The Disease Concept of Alcoholism*. New Haven: College and University Press, in association with Hillhouse Press, New Brunswick, N.J.: 1960.

Johnson, Vernon. *I'll Quit Tomorrow*. New York: Harper Collins Publishers, 1980.

Intervention. Minneapolis: Johnson Institute, 1986.

Jones, Thomas A. *Mind Change: The Overcomer's Handbook*. Woburn, Mass.: Discipleship Publications International, 1994.

Keller, John E. *Ministering to Alcoholics*. Minneapolis: Angsbury Publishing House, 1966.

Kissin, Benjamin and Bebleiter, Henri. *The Biology of Alcoholism: The Pathogenesis of Alcoholism—Biological Factors*. New York: Plenum Press, 1983.

Kubler-Ross, Elisabeth. *On Death and Dying*. New York: Collier Books, 1969.

Kurtz, Ernst. *Not God*. Center City, Minn.: Hazelden Foundation, 1979.

Laing, Sam and Laing, Geri. *Friends and Lovers*. Woburn, Mass.: Discipleship Publications International, 1996.

Leipold, William. *Walk Through the Valley*. Independence, Mo.: Independence Press, 1975.

Martin, Father Joseph. *No Laughing Matter*. New York: Harper and Row, 1982.

Milan, James and Ketchann, Katherine. *Under the Influence: A Guide to the Myths and Realities of Alcoholism*. Seattle: Madrone Publishers, 1981.

Mooney, Al J. *The Recovery Book*. New York: Publishers, Inc., 1992.

O'Neill, John and O'Neill, Pat. *Concerned Intervention*. Oakland, Calif.: New Harbinger Publishers, Inc., 1992.

Parenting for Prevention. Minneapolis: Johnson Institute, 1995.

Polson, Beth and Newton, Miller. *Not My Kid*. New York: Avon Books, 1984.

Sandmaier, Marian. *The Invisible Alcoholics: Women and Alcohol*. Blue Ridge Summit, Penn.: Human Services Institute and TAB Books, 1992.

Schaffer, Dick. *Choices and Consequences*. Minneapolis: Johnson Institute, 1987.

Schucket, Mark, M.D. *Drug and Alcohol Abuse: A Clinical Guide to Diagnosis and Treatment*. New York: Plenum Publishing Corp., 1989.

Silvous, Jan. *Please Don't Say You Need Me*. Grand Rapids, Mich.: Zondervan Publications, 1989.

Taliaferro, Mike. *The Lion Never Sleeps*. Woburn, Mass.: Discipleship Publications International, 1996.

Tiebout, Henry S. "Surrender Versus Compliance in Therapy with Special Reference to Alcoholism." *Quarterly Journal of Studies on Alcoholism*. Vol. 14, No. 1, (March, 1953): 56-68.

"Tobacco, Alcohol and Illicit Drug Deaths." NY State Office of Alcohol and Substance Abuse Services. New York: June 19, 1995, p. 32-37.

Wilmes, David. *Alcohol is a Drug Too: What Happens to Kids When We're Afraid to Say No*. Minneapolis: Johnson Institute, 1993.

Who Are We?

Discipleship Publications International (DPI) began publishing in 1993. We are a nonprofit Christian publisher affiliated with the International Churches of Christ, committed to publishing and distributing materials that honor God, lift up Jesus Christ and show how his message practically applies to all areas of life. We have a deep conviction that no one changes life like Jesus and that the implementation of his teaching will revolutionize any life, any marriage, any family and any singles household.

Since our beginning we have published more than 100 titles; plus we have produced a number of important, spiritual audio products. More than one million volumes have been printed, and our works have been translated into more than a dozen languages—international is not just a part of our name! Our books are shipped regularly to every inhabited continent.

To see a more detailed description of our works, find us on the World Wide Web at www.dpibooks.org. You can order books by calling 1-888-DPI-BOOK 24 hours a day. From outside the US, call 978-670-8840 during Boston-area business hours.

We appreciate the hundreds of comments we have received from readers. We would love to hear from you. Here are other ways to get in touch:

Mail: DPI, 2 Sterling Road, Billerica, Mass. 01862
E-mail: dpibooks@icoc.org

Find us on the World Wide Web

www.dpibooks.org
1-888-DPI-BOOK